those around you, then be sure you don't read this book. But if you want to find a balm for your unhealed wounds, insight into your unhealthy obsessions, and courage to pursue your unfulfilled dreams, then take a sit and read.

Nancy Guthrie, author of *Holding on to Hope, The One Year Book of Hope, Hoping for Something Better, Dinner Table Devotions, Hearing Jesus Speak Into Your Sorrow,* and *When Your Family's Lost a Loved One* and the *Seeing Jesus in the Old Testament* Bible Study series

Over the years, I have encountered countless men, young and old, whose lives intersected at some point with Bill Delvaux. The common denominator is that each one of them can trace back to that intersection, and talk about a shift that took place. That shift involved something he said, or some kind of experience with Bill where they were stirred, invited into something bigger and changed in some way.

You are about to experience that intersection. Prepare to be invited, stirred and disrupted in the best of ways.

David Thomas, therapist and author of *Wild Things: The Art of Nurturing Boys*

I've known Bill as a great teacher with a passion for truth, God's Word, and authentic faith at the school my children attend. What I never really knew before reading his book was the rich story that's shaped him and his heart to make him the man that he is and is becoming. It is a rare gift when someone opens the book of themselves to share their deepest stories as Bill has done and I believe those who read his story will be grateful as I am.

Steven Curtis Chapman, Grammy and Dove Award-winning singer and songwriter

Bill Delvaux fiercely taps into the heart of every person's struggle to write their own story. The experiences he so honestly and vulnerably shares from his own story are as penetrating as they are inspiring and redeeming.

Jake Speck, theatre producer and actor in the Broadway hit *Jersey Boys* and the TV series *Nashville*

It's rare to find a friend these days who isn't just ready to tell you the answers, but instead, encourages you to ask the questions. Bill Delvaux is that kind of friend, and he has written that kind of book. As he traces his path with disarming transparency, I am drawn in. I am caught up. I want more. I highly recommend *Landmarks*.

Brown Bannister, Grammy award-winning producer

To me, Bill is something of an evangelical exotic: the rare male who is genuinely willing to be transparent and authentic in light of the gospel and its invitation to be transformed. I sat in Bill's classes many times over the years as he developed the themes in this book through teaching and relating his own story. I gained plenty and am glad to know that many more will have the same opportunity.

Ashley Cleveland, Grammy and Dove Award Winning Recording Artist

I commend Bill Delvaux's new work, *Landmarks* to you. I have the privilege of serving as pastor to the church where Bill and Heidi are members, and have witnessed first-hand the impact of this book's concepts on hundreds of people. Take this book up, read it, and share it with others. You'll be glad that you did.

Scott Sauls, Senior Pastor of Christ Presbyterian Church, Nashville TN

God has given Bill a special platform and unique gift set and his message in *Landmarks* is powerful, inspiring, and impactful. I have watched for many years the way God has used Bill to impact so many people. I am thankful for his investment in my life, and I am grateful to call him my friend, brother, and mentor.

Drew Maddux, former Vanderbilt basketball star and head basketball coach at Christ Presbyterian Academy

What a gift *Landmarks* is! With his first book, Bill Delvaux has given us the beauty of God's redemptive story; the fruit of his own well-stewarded pain; and a path for each of us to follow into a journey of grace, healing, and freedom. I cannot wait to see how God is going to use this book in the lives of countless men—to help them find their place in God's story.

Scotty Smith, founding pastor, Christ Community Church and author of *Every Day Prayers: 365 Days to a Gospel Centered Faith, Objects of His Affection, The Reign of Grace* and *Restoring Broken Things*

Bill Delvaux has incredible insight into the journey we need to take. I recommend this book as one that is filled with wisdom and profound encouragement. Read it with an open heart and an expectation that God will use it mightily to transform you.

Carter Crenshaw, senior pastor of West End Community Church

In *Landmarks*, Bill Delvaux lays out the spiritual journey we all find ourselves on, but rarely wake up to see. Through his vulnerability and his conversational teaching, he helps lift the fog of religion and boredom and invites us all to re-imagine the mark of God in our pain, thrills, shame, and suffering.

Xan Hood, author of Sweat, Blood, and Tears:
What God Uses to Make a Man

He always went beyond his job to get to know his students—meeting guys one on one during his lunch hour, hosting Bible studies at his home on weekends, literally running alongside me (member of his cross country team) and still having the breath to engage me with his wisdom and his questions.

Ben, 29

Mr. Delvaux taught me how to begin to see my own presuppositions and assumptions about the world around me. He challenged me to look at life and faith from new and truly biblical angles.

Betsie, 29

Mr. Delvaux exemplifies what it is to be a man of God. He helped show me the doorway that led to my adventures with Jesus. He is still the best teacher I have ever had.

Ben, 21

Coach D woke me up to the truth of this life. His method wasn't jarring and shaking, and it certainly wasn't breakfast in bed. He simply flipped on the light switch as if to say, "It's time to see."

Mark, 25

BILL DELVAUX

LANDMARKS

VACANCY

TURNING POINTS
ON YOUR JOURNEY
TOWARD GOD

B&H
PUBLISHING GROUP
Nashville, Tennessee

978-1-4336-7922-3

Published by B&H Publishing Group
Nashville, Tennessee

Dewey Decimal Classification: 248.84
Subject Heading: CHRISTIAN LIFE \ DISCIPLESHIP \
SPIRITUAL LIFE

1 2 3 4 5 6 7 8 9 • 16 15 14 13

To Heidi, without whom I would have
never begun this journey.

CONTENTS

ACKNOWLEDGMENTS

No book is a solitary task. This one is no exception. There are so many who have helped make it a reality. Here are some of the main ones that come to mind.

Thanks to Nancy Guthrie, who first suggested to me the idea of becoming a writer. Sadly, I ignored her encouragement for a long time, but the seed was planted.

Thanks to John Thompson, who, several years later, encouraged me again to write. This time I listened.

Thanks to David Huffman, my agent, who took the shards of my attempted book proposal and turned it into something compelling.

Thanks to Matt West, the acquisitions editor. You took a big risk on me by being the original champion of this book. I hope it does not disappoint.

Thanks to Dawn Woods, my editor, who gave me so much freedom as a new author.

Thanks to Kim Stanford and Diana Lawrence for the layout and design. You made this book look so much better than I ever dreamed it could be.

Thanks to the publicity team at B&H, to Patrick Bonner, David Schrader, Robin Patterson, and David Myers. I have appreciated your hard work in getting this book out.

Thanks to my Sunday school class at Christ Presbyterian Church, who listened to the ideas of this book as they first came out. Your feedback and encouragement was immensely helpful. Thank you for believing in me.

Thanks to the hundreds of high school students at Christ Presbyterian Academy whom I have known over the years. You have taught me to connect the truths of the Bible into the terrible abyss that lies in the human heart.

Thanks especially to my Men in the Bible class at the school. Your willingness to talk about the hard things as young men is so life-giving.

Thanks to many cherished authors from past and present, some of whom are quoted in this book. Their words have shaped me in ways too deep at times to understand, much less describe.

Thanks to the countless men who have shared their stories with me and deeply enriched my life.

Thanks to my band of brothers, Matt, Bruce, Bob, and Carter. You have given me the strength to press through the hard places.

Thanks to my Sunday night small group. Life together with you is opening new doors in my heart.

Thanks to the board of Landmark Journey Ministries. You all gave me the courage to jump off the cliff and follow my passion.

Thanks to Kit and Tricia McDermott. The five days spent with you has changed so many things for Heidi and I.

Thank you, Rachel, for reading every word and making insightful suggestions. You are not just a great editor. You are a hero to your mom and I.

Thank you, Abigail, for your words of encouragement as I wrote. Your name means "my father's delight," and you have lived that out so well.

Finally, thank you, Heidi, for giving me hours on end as I wrote and wrote and rewrote. Your love for me over the years has been amazing.

Soli Deo Gloria.

FOREWORD

People mark their territory. Always have and always will. We either leave the place better than we found it, or worse, but never the same.

Kilroy, that handy mythical man who shows up as a comic wherever he is needed, might well symbolize those who have not yet found their way in the goodness of grace and truth. Kilroy *was* here, but isn't here now. Much of modern life is like the cartoon . . . a man with a long nose and sad, curious eyes peeking over the wall, hiding, silent, and unengaged except as an observer, another stick figure in the passing drama but not actually alive here inside the story.

Landmarks is the narrative of a man who refused to live outside the sphere of life, or in the isolation to which his sorrows and despair had consigned him. Uncertain, afraid, but willing to risk his marred self-identity for the possibility of a new way of living, Bill began a difficult multi-decade struggle in the presence of a few friends to emerge in manhood as a brother, friend and counselor to those on a similar journey out of silence and into the rich essence of life.

Bill's premise, and mine, is that your story matters—the good, the bad, and the ugly. All of it. The treasure of your life cannot be found or measured without a truthful narrative, yours, told first to yourself in spirit and in truth, and then to others who wish to accept the invitation to participate in the fresh new life of the Holy Spirit, which God has designed for us all.

Wes Yoder, author of *Bond of Brothers*

INTRODUCTION

Midway along the journey of our life I woke to find myself in a
dark wood for I had wandered off from the straight path.

—DANTE

Out of the depths I call to you, O LORD!

—PSALM 130:1 NIV

It was just another typical afternoon on a typical summer day. But not for me. Everything in my life was about to change.

It was my turn to feed our infant daughter. She had been born with some physical issues that made each feeding an hour-long affair, so I had lots of time for thinking and praying. And I needed it. Shortly before her birth, I had resigned as the pastor of a church I had planted a few years earlier, and I was unsure of the next step. But this

1

was no momentary bump in my ministry career. This was a cataclysmic quake. I was falling apart.

Like most young ministers, I had dreamed of a successful church, both in terms of numbers and impact. I was convinced that God had called me to it, but now the dream was crushed. And with the crushing appeared a larger foe, one that I had kept at bay for years—depression. It was beginning to swallow me whole. I became morose, aloof, and angry. My marriage was struggling as well, for my depression put Heidi on edge, and she felt she had to prop me up all the time. I was also furious with God. I had given my life to do His work, and my reward for such obedience appeared to be failure and now despair.

At the time of my resignation, I had graciously been given six months of severance pay. It was supposed to allow me some time to heal and get redirected. But I was now three months in, and there was no healing, nor was there any redirection.

Instead, that afternoon the crushing weight of despair pushed me down into complete darkness. As I continued to feed my daughter, I thought briefly about suicide. But I brushed that thought away. I understood only too well the devastation suicide brings to those who are close to the victim. I could never inflict that kind of sadness on Heidi or my children. So I continued to sit in the darkness, and out of that abyss I suddenly cried out, "God, I don't care what it takes. I want out of this!"

It was the moment that would change everything. My journey out of the abyss began.

For the next seventeen years, I wandered frequently and wondered at times exactly where I was heading. Sometimes I ended up circling back and revisiting places I thought I had moved past. At other times, with no clear bearings to orient myself, I just felt lost. But at many unexpected points along the way, God appeared and gently guided me forward.

During those years, I took a job as a teacher and coach at a Christian high school where I had to find a way to connect the Bible to the hearts of students. In the process, I found my own heart connecting to Scripture in new ways. I was slowly climbing out of the abyss.

One day as I was talking with my good friend Daniel, the high school counselor, I began to describe some of the places I had traveled in my journey. He asked me to write them down and send the list to him. I first entitled it "Mile Markers," like the ones posted along the interstate. Heidi objected to the name because she thought it made the journey sound too safe and predictable. She was right. This was no leisurely drive; this was a trek through the wilderness.

About the same time, I was reading *Undaunted Courage*, the harrowing account of the Lewis and Clark expedition. These two men and their crew oared upstream for months to find the source of the Missouri

River, hoping to discover a waterway across America to the Pacific. All along the way, they kept mentioning certain landmarks they had to reach, even if the exact path wasn't known. Then it clicked. That's exactly what I had felt in my journey, an awareness of certain landmarks I had to reach even if I didn't know how I was going to get there. And so the "Landmarks" idea was born.

What exactly are the landmarks? Everyone knows at some level that life is a journey. It is a deep-seated feeling born out of the experience of change and growth. We are not what we were ten years ago, nor will we be the same ten years from now. But therein lies the problem. What kind of journey is this? Where am I going? How do I even know if this is the right direction? What if I'm lost? Not only do we have a sense that life is a journey, we also sense that we're missing the map and some basic orienteering skills.

Here is where the landmarks come into play. Think of them as points that chart out a journey we all need to take if we want to live well. It's like looking at a topographical map, one that has the mountains and streams and forests marked on it, but little else. We have enough to get started on the hike, but there are still many unknowns ahead. Or imagine driving a car across America on some of the old highways with only a roadmap and no available Internet. We may know the general direction forward, but there are still many questions. What will we encounter on the road? Where will we stay each night? That's the feel for the landmarks.

The Bible also speaks of life as a journey. Jesus Himself laid out the general direction of the path ahead: "If anyone wants to be My follower, he must deny himself, take up his cross, and follow Me" (Mark 8:34). We are immediately struck by the thought that something needs to die in order to take this journey. Interestingly, the apostle Paul marked out the same trail: "I have been crucified with Christ and I no longer live, but Christ lives in me" (Gal. 2:19–20). It seems that the key to finding the life we long for is submitting to the death we fear. For what we most desire is hidden underneath our deepest terror. This is the course set by the nine landmarks in this book (see diagram on the next page). The first four chart a downward descent into what feels like death. It's a crucifixion, agonizing at times. The fifth landmark is a pivot in the journey, turning us in the opposite direction. The final four describe the resurrection we can now enter into, an ascent into *real* life. We are finally becoming what we were meant to be.

> It seems that the key to finding the life we long for is submitting to the death we fear. For what we most desire is hidden underneath our deepest terror.

As I have spoken about these landmarks to many, I have had to be painfully honest. After all, they trace out my own journey. They represent my climb out of the abyss. But the feedback has surprised me. So many have spoken of a deep connection to what I have experienced.

A wise counselor once told me, "What is most personal is most universal." And so, what is written here is offered in the hope that this journey can be yours also.

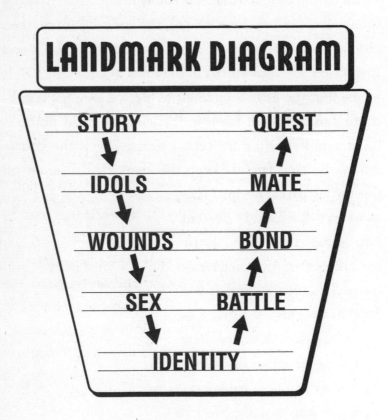

6

Part One

DESCENDING INTO DEATH

Then the Old Man of the Earth stooped over the floor of the
cave, raised a huge stone from it, and left it leaning. It disclosed
a great hole that went plumb-down.
"That is the way," he said.
"But there are no stairs."
"You must throw yourself in. There is no other way."

—GEORGE MACDONALD, *THE GOLDEN KEY*

Landmark #1

STORY

History is a story written by the finger of God.
—C. S. Lewis

I had always felt life first as a story:
and if there is a story there is a storyteller.
—G. K. Chesterton

For once in my life, I was not looking forward to going to the movies. It was Christmas Day, and one of our family traditions has always been to watch a film together after opening presents. But this time I let my daughters, Abigail and Rachel, choose the movie. After scanning the paper, they decided on one I had not heard anything about, *Finding Neverland*. When Heidi, my wife, told me that it had some connection to Peter Pan, my heart sank. *Another Peter Pan movie*, I said to myself. *And I didn't even like the first one Disney made*. But trying to be the good and dutiful father, I didn't object. This one was for the kids, so I decided to grit my teeth and endure it.

After finding our seats in the theater, I began to wonder how much of a sleeper this was going to be. Maybe I would be entertained a bit. Then again, maybe not. The lights went down, and the story began. However, soon into the movie, my dread shifted to growing interest. This was no cartoon or fairy tale. This was the real life story of James Barrie, the author of *Peter Pan*.

I found myself drawn into the tension and tragedy of the story. I watched as the opening night of Barrie's latest play in London ended as a complete flop. I saw his miserable marriage come slowly unglued. Then I watched his growing interest in a fatherless family of four boys whom he met one day at a park. I was saddened at the sickness of the boys' mom, a sickness that soon became terminal. And I was especially mesmerized by one of the boys, Peter, who wrestled with grief, first over his father and now his mother. Finally I began to realize that the story of *Peter Pan* is really the story of Barrie's lost childhood and his longing to find it again. By the closing scene, I was so completely disarmed that my tears began to flow. When the final credits rolled, I didn't want to leave my seat. For something wonderfully unsettling had just happened. I had been ambushed by a movie.

Later, as I tried to put words to what had happened to me in the theater, I realized that I had subconsciously put myself into the story of James Barrie. I saw some of my own marital struggles in his. I saw my own inability to grieve losses similar to his incapacity. I saw my own maneuvers to avoid pain parallel his. But it was the boy Peter who completely undid me. He had found the courage to speak his anger, traverse his sadness, and find his heart again. Peter showed me the road I knew I must take even though I had no idea how to start. During those two hours at the theater, I had connected my own story to theirs—both Barrie's and Peter's—in a way that brought insight and ignited desire. It was a defining moment.

Such is the power of story.

Think about the last talk or sermon you heard. What do you remember? You can probably recall a story, if one was told, for story is the thing we retain long after ideas and concepts slip from our memory. Why is this so? Because we do not live our lives as ideas or concepts. We live them as a story. And when stories are told, we find ourselves identifying with the characters and learning from them in ways we simply cannot do with concepts. But the

> Story is the thing we retain long after ideas and concepts slip from our memory.

power of story reaches even further, for concepts only speak to the mind. They can deliver some needed information, but beyond that, they offer no help. Yet we need so much more. We need our hearts engaged. We need to come alive.

So we find ourselves always looking for a story to connect with, one that can speak to the sadness and joy we feel, one that can help us interpret the complexity of our lives and give us the eyes to see and the strength to press forward. Without such a story, we will play it safe with our hearts, stuck in a routine. Or we will wither under the confusion in our lives, unable to make sense of the chaos in us and around us. For story is not only powerful; it is foundational.

This is our first landmark: find a good story and steer toward it.

Missing the Story

But where can we find such a story? For we now live in the postmodern age where there seems to be no overarching story to which we can hitch our lives. Students no longer go to college to discover a universal story or system of truth. Instead, they receive diversity instruction, claiming that all options are valid, all philosophical frameworks are equal. And it gets no better after college. Here we are confronted with endless media images, gigabytes of information, and very, very frantic lives. We are left to wade through the noise of it all and cobble together our own story. With no remaining super-story to believe in, we are left to construct the meaning of our own lives as best we can.

So where do we go? I know where I went for a number of years. It wasn't the TV or the computer. It wasn't even good books. And it wasn't the church either. I went to the movies.

There, for a couple of hours, I would find myself being lifted up and out of the doldrums of my fragmented life and into something that stirred me. The movies gave me perspective and sometimes a hero to emulate. Best of all, they would fire my heart in a way that left me aching for more. At least in the ache I knew I was alive. (It's no surprise that I ended up buying *Finding Neverland* to watch again.)

Generally, my experience with movies had seemed more defining than my experience at church. But I had no idea why. I was certainly connecting to the stories portrayed on the screen, but I was missing the biggest story of all. Ironically, I was missing it even though I had been reading the story for years. The title of this story? The Bible.

> My experience with movies had seemed more defining than my experience at church.

The title itself held a missing clue for me, for the word *Bible* is just a rendering of the Greek word for "book." But I had really not been reading it as a book at all, and that's why I was missing the story it told.

In my earlier years, I approached the Bible as a first-aid kit, the place I went to when I needed a bandage to cover a wound or medicine to ease my pain. If I felt anxious, I'd find a verse about peace. If I felt rejected, I'd seek out a promise about God's love and acceptance. But as I got older and more intellectually aware, the Bible also became a pantry of ideas. I would hunt through it to construct theologies that had the most rational appeal, or I would search it to find principles that I could articulate. In my preaching or teaching, I would pull out the can marked "Justification," or the jar labeled "God's Holiness," or the container filled with ideas for a good marriage. But after using them, I would put them back in the pantry and return to the familiar state that often denied what I had just taught. I could deliver the goods to others, but had no idea how to take them in myself. Remember, concepts speak to the mind but cannot enter into the deep places of the heart. My repeated return to the old self was proof of this. It was frustrating beyond words.

There is nothing necessarily wrong with these approaches to the Bible. It is certainly a book of profound comfort and a storehouse of deep truth, but these are insufficient for what we really ache for—a story. And this is where both approaches miss the most obvious point of all, the one that I missed for years: the Bible presents itself as a story. Like any good story, it has a beginning: "In the beginning God created the heavens and the earth" (Gen. 1:1). And like many great stories, it has a happy ending: "Death will no longer exist; grief, crying, and pain will exist no longer" (Rev. 21:4). In the middle is the stuff of great drama, where evil strikes savagely and where beauty wins despite terrible odds, all with a cast of characters as strange and beguiling as any movie I've ever seen. And yet this is no script; these things actually happened. Story and history are fused.

This aroused hope in me. Perhaps what I felt in the movies I could also feel in real life.

More clues about the Bible as story then began to surface. I discovered that the familiar time line we use in our history books is not something to be assumed. The idea that time is linear, that it moves like a story, is such a basic viewpoint that we do not think there is any other way to look at it. But many cultures, both ancient and modern, have actually thought of time in a circular fashion. Experiencing the seasons and observing the movement of heavenly bodies seemed to justify the belief to these cultures that time is a cycle of endless repetition. However, in vivid contrast, the Bible presents time as a line with a distinct beginning and end, the way we think of stories. The Bible lays a unique linear framework for all storytelling.

I then ran across another clue that really excited me. One day I happened to read an account of how Easter and Christmas were dramatized in the medieval church. Eventually these plays became too long for a church service, and they were moved outside. And then someone got the idea to make a play about the whole story of the Bible and perform it as a way to teach the Scriptures in a world where reading and books were rare. Troupes of actors would travel the landscape and perform these so-called mystery plays in villages and towns. They eventually became the foundation of our modern form of drama, made famous by Shakespeare. And from this came a new version for our technological age, the movies.

> The very act of making and watching movies owes a considerable debt to the Bible. It is not only a mega-story to live in; it is also the foundation for all the movies I have ever wanted to live in.

I had hit something. The very act of making and watching movies owes a considerable debt to the Bible. It is not only a mega-story to live in; it is also the foundation for all the movies I have ever wanted to live in.

Writing My Own Story

Although putting all of this together was interesting and even confirming for me, it did not necessarily move me toward the landmark. The story of my life was still disconnected from God's story at a heart level. I felt stuck in neutral, unable to get traction and move forward.

As I was struggling, I uncovered the real obstacle. It wasn't understanding the Bible as story, but in how I was choosing to see the story of my life. All of us to one degree or another disconnect from God's story because we are fundamentally committed to being the author of our own stories. Actually, we attempt to do something even more grandiose and irrational. We not only author our own story, but also try to direct it, produce it, and play the lead role. We justify this as perfectively acceptable because we think we know what's best for us. Scripting our own story keeps us in control so that we can gain what we think we need. But the story never really ends up going very well. Things happen that mess up our carefully constructed plans, and our attempts to rewrite the script in order to clean up the mess only complicate things further. Frustration degenerates into desperation. Desperation finally yields to despair. At its best, our story parallels a depressing soap opera. At worst, it becomes a tragedy.

This is what my life has felt like.

Ever since my college days, I have wanted to play some notable role, to do something that mattered. I wanted to cut my mark in the tree; I wanted to blaze a trail that would forever change others. Now combine that ache with another that was even more imperative to me: affirmation. I needed it. No, that is way too weak. I *craved* it like a thirsty man in the final stages of dehydration. I had to have it. Everything depended on my heart finding the validation that made me feel loved, wanted, understood, and appreciated. After struggling with a number of career options that offered little relief for the ache, I discovered the ministry in my early twenties. There I found both significance and validation. It sealed the deal. That was going to be my life story.

I went on to seminary and landed in youth ministry, where I made another discovery: I could teach. I could communicate in such a way that I could make a mark with my words and then bask in the affirmation of my listeners. It tasted like honey to me. The irony of this was that I was a minister. I was supposedly doing this for God. At least I believed that at the time, but honesty now tells a different tale. I was really doing it because this way of writing my story seemed to work. It offered what I needed and gave me a sense of control. But lurking underneath was a mass of unsorted pain from my adolescence that I never wanted to examine. This sorrow felt so out of control that I kept running from it by doing ministry. And the tale only got more frustrating when I landed a job teaching and coaching at a Christian high school where the same subconscious script writing appeared again.

I came to be known as an excellent teacher and a successful running coach. This massaged the deep ache I had been feeling. I was stroked for my ability to impact students, and I kept at it fast and furious. Only this time it was my success that undid me. For once I began to hang my soul's validation on my performance as a teacher and coach, it no longer felt like a massage. It became pressure. Each day in class meant a new attempt to gain the affirmation of my students. Each athletic event became a new pressure point of meeting expectations as a coach. What I depended on to affirm me had to be jump-started each day like a cranky old car. And I feared that one day the car wouldn't start. Then I would be seen as a nothing, a zero, a failure.

This is so often the case when we write the stories of our lives. The self-constructed narratives work for a while, but the wheels begin to come off at some point. The plot line that seems to offer us so much freedom turns and begins to strangle us. However, the idea

> All of us to one degree or another disconnect from God's story because we are fundamentally committed to being the author of our own stories.

that I was scripting my own story, and that it was slowly killing me simply didn't register. I was blind to it. Nor could I see that what I really ached for was something that only God could offer me. But I couldn't shake the compulsion to keep writing my story even with attempts to do better or try harder. My frustration had long passed desperation and was approaching despair.

Understanding the Plot

Every movie or book has at least one key theme or idea it is trying to communicate. This is the message of the story, the foundational belief that becomes the controlling vision for the plot. We are no different in our own heart stories. There is some theme, some deep belief that controls the story we are attempting to write. And this core theme is formed not by clear, objective thinking but by a reaction to pain. In the wounding we find the theme. This was so true for me.

> In the wounding we find the theme. This was so true for me.

When I was finally able to put words to my theme, this is what came out:

Never, ever fail in front of others.

This mantra had been formed out of shame-filled experiences of failure and abandonment. There was the time in seventh grade when I was called upon to play basketball for an intramural team, but I couldn't deliver because I had never been coached. I didn't even know the rules. There was further failure in sports as I struggled to make it on the tennis team, only to find myself losing key matches in front of my coach and teammates. In track, the same pattern held. I was successful in the sprints until a couple of other runners started passing me in the 400 Meter. I didn't know how to handle the failure, so I just quit.

My failures continued to pile up, reinforcing the theme with terrible precision. I got blackballed from a fraternity, I went nowhere as a recording artist, and I failed as a church planter. The pain of failing in front of others, of not delivering the goods, drove me to find things that I did well. I would perfect them on my own and then perform them in front of others to get that rush of affirmation.

> I didn't know how to handle the failure, so I just quit.

This was the theme that I kept writing and living. How could I ever get out of my own constricting story and connect to God's?

Into the Unknown

There is one general movement we all must make when we begin to enter God's story, and one that we must continue to do in ever deepening ways. We need to let go and submit. We need to let go of our role as author and director and submit to God. The book of Hebrews sets up this movement in a stirring and unforgettable way. In chapter 11 we find a roll call of characters from the Old Testament who decided to connect to God's story. They did this by letting go, submitting, and keeping faith in God and in the story He was telling. There was no formula for what then happened. Some were famous, while others were complete unknowns. Some became point persons for God's redemptive work while others seemed to play only minor roles. Some of their stories resemble films I would love to be in: "who . . . shut the mouths of lions, quenched the raging of fire, escaped the edge of the sword, gained strength after being weak, became mighty in battle, and put foreign armies to flight" (vv. 33–34). But others are more like grisly war movies that make me queasy: "They were stoned, they were sawed in two, they died by the sword, they wandered about in sheepskins, in goatskins, destitute, afflicted, and mistreated" (v. 37).

So which role do we get if we let go and submit to God? Not one whisper of an answer is offered. Instead, this is what we get: "Let us lay aside every weight and the sin that so easily ensnares us, and run with endurance the race that lies before us" (12:1). We are simply asked to set the blocks, take our marks, and run the race that God chooses to give us. We hesitate and wonder, *Can we trust Him? What might He ask us to do? Where will it take us?* It all seems so unpredictable. It seems so unknown. It *is* unknown.

But some encouragement is given to us even if clear answers aren't. In the same passage in Hebrews, we are told, "Let us fix our eyes on Jesus, the author and perfecter of our faith, who for the joy set before him endured the cross, scorning its shame, and sat down at the right hand of the throne of God" (12:2 NIV). Here the Author of our faith does something unimaginable: He writes Himself into His own story. This is something along the line of what Alfred Hitchcock used to do in his movies by making an appearance somewhere in each film. But the role Jesus casts for Himself is no cameo; it is the worst possible part imaginable. He writes Himself into a story where He is misunderstood, rejected, denounced, mocked, beaten, tortured, and finally killed in the most degrading and disgusting manner known at the time. And that's not the worst of it. In that death He chooses to carry all the pain and sorrow of all our rebellious attempts at authoring our own stories. Then He holds out His hand and says, "You are going to have to trust that the role I am writing for you is good, not just good in the story I am writing, but good for you also." And we begin to wonder if perhaps we can trust Him because of how He has written His own part. He endured the worst. Maybe the role He wants us to play is the best for us after all.

But there is more here. Jesus was able to endure the worst precisely because He knew that this was not the end of the story. The same passage in Hebrews says that He kept the joy of what was coming set before Him. It was the joy of triumph, the joy of accomplishing something grueling yet wonderful, and most importantly, the joy of returning to His beloved Father. Seeing the end gave Jesus perspective and passion in His most horrific moments. Incidentally, this is also why all those before Him in the Old Testament chose to play their roles; they sensed something way beyond the confines of their present lives. They did not expect or demand that this life would bring everything their hearts longed for; instead, they could trust that God would bring their story to a joyful ending. And of course it is the same for us. We can stay in the role given to us even when things get terribly dark, for this is not

> Then He holds out his hand and says, "You are going to have to trust that the role I am writing for you is good, not just good in the story I am writing, but good for you also."

24

the end of the story. There is a great good coming that we can set our hearts on.

Personal Coaching

This general motion toward God's story must be personalized, for each of us has our own story we've attempted to write. Each of us has our own individual themes, our own sadnesses, and our own fears. Learning to submit to God's story means allowing Him to come and touch our own heart in a way that releases us to play our role. He doesn't just hand us the script; He wants to empower us to act.

Let's go back to the core theme that paralyzed me: "Never, ever fail in front of others." I began to realize that failure was so defining because it had become my identity. It was the irrevocable sentence on my soul: if I failed, then I was a failure. No wonder I ran from it. I had no one to walk me through failure or interpret it for me. I never had a coach.

Ah, I was on to something here. I began to realize that this was exactly what God wanted to do for me. He wanted to be my coach through the Holy Spirit. Romans 8:15 began to speak to me: "For you did not receive a spirit of slavery to fall back into fear, but you received the Spirit of adoption, by whom we cry out, 'Abba, Father!'" The Holy Spirit wanted to coach me into the truth that I am a son. I am not on my own, nor do I need to be a slave to the fear of failure. Who I am is treasured far more than my daily performance. This verse and others like it took on a life and power I had never known before, for I was now allowing them to touch my story and speak into it.

As good as this was, there was still more. This was not just about lopping off a set of false beliefs and replacing them with new ones. This was—and is—about connecting to God Himself, about God entering our fallen stories and personally calling us out of them. I will never forget the first time I sensed the Father asking me, "Will you let Me coach you?" I could feel the tears come from some very deep and abandoned place inside of me as I simply nodded and whispered, "Yes, I would love You to." He really wanted to do that for me, not just so I could play my role well, but because He loves me as a son. What good father doesn't want to coach his son through life? As I began to believe that, I found that I was able to take more risks. Failure still hurt at times, but it seemed much less shattering, much less precarious. It mattered to me far less about how I performed in class on any particular day or what someone thought of me. What mattered to me was that I mattered to God. This no longer felt like a dive into the void, but more like an adventure with a trusted friend.

In the children's movie *The NeverEnding Story*, a grieving boy who has recently lost his mom borrows a strange volume from a bookstore owner who claims that it is dangerous. Drawn in by the warning, the boy opens the book and starts to read the story of a young warrior sent on a perilous quest to save a kingdom by finding a new name for its young queen. As the story progresses, the boy gets drawn further and further into it until he is startled to learn that he has a part in the story, for he knows the name that can save the queen. And it is none other than the name of his dead mother. In a climactic moment, he decides to scream her name, only to find himself physically sucked into the very story he had only been reading.

> What mattered to me was that I mattered to God. This no longer felt like a dive into the void, but more like an adventure with a trusted friend.

When you pick up the Bible, remember that it is a dangerous book, for you are being asked to let go and enter the story. And if you get sucked in, there is no telling what may happen.

Landmark #2

IDOLS

If man was not made for God, why is he only happy in God?
If man was made for God, why is he so opposed to God?

—Blaise Pascal

Man's nature, so to speak, is a perpetual factory of idols.

—John Calvin

It was a phone call that led to a treasure hunt. My father informed me that my great-uncle had been put into a nursing home. He had been found alone in a hotel room after moving out of the office he'd been using as a living space. Although that scenario was intriguing, what really caught my attention was the next piece of news. He had instructed the family to go through his house and take anything they wanted.

29

But you see, this was no ordinary house. It was a two-hundred-year-old structure, only the second home built in the entire town. Inside was the treasure: room after room of coveted antiques.

When my family gathered on the chosen day, we eagerly discussed what gems we would discover. The thrill of the hunt was on despite having been warned that my great-uncle was a hoarder. But nothing could have prepared us for our first glimpse.

As we opened the back door into the kitchen, we had to immediately step up onto a three-foot platform of trash packed down so tightly that we could walk on top of it. When we moved into the dining room, things got more precarious. We had to step up onto more trash and boxes only to find ourselves maneuvering across the top of the dining room table.

The rest of the house was more of the same, room after room stuffed with trash, mail, documents, unopened purchases, books, clothes, and trinkets bought from local department stores. Tucked here and there among the piles of debris, we managed to find the antique gems: roomy wooden armoires, marble-topped serving pieces, ornamental dressers, large decorative frames, and classic lawyer bookcases.

Next came the challenge of extracting our treasures from the rubbish. As we climbed and crawled through the house pulling the furniture out, the conversation kept circling back to my great-uncle. How could he live like this? What was going on inside of him? As a bachelor, he hadn't let anyone in the house for years. Now we knew why. But the story grew sadder as we learned that after he trashed the house, he moved into his office where he repeated the same troubling way of life. He was finally forced to take up residence in the hotel room where he had been found suffering from pneumonia.

On further investigation, we discovered that each room contained a different decade of trash, as if he had filled up one room before moving on to the next. When the house was finally cleaned out, enough trash was shoveled out of the kitchen alone to fill a large Dumpster. How does anyone get like this? How can someone become so attached to things that he can't let go of anything, even trash? We were baffled as well as repulsed by what we saw.

This same kind of attachment is explored in epic terms in Tolkien's famous work *Lord of the Rings*. The plot centers on the one ring of power that sucks everyone who sees it into its grip. It pretends to offer power, strength, and mastery over others, but in the end all it gives is corruption, torment, and death. Once you try to own the ring, it owns you. Once you take it, it takes you. Everyone feels its

> Once you try to own the ring, it owns you. Once you take it, it takes you.

hypnotic pull, but can anyone resist it long enough to destroy it? That's the pivotal question around which the story develops.

What I saw in my great-uncle and what Tolkien presents with the ring provide the backdrop for the second landmark. For once we begin to submit to God's story and let Him write our role in His script, we become painfully aware of all the trinkets we have grabbed onto as props in our own stories. We saw in the last landmark how we *ran away from* God. Now we begin to see all the things we *run to* instead. And it's not a casual connection we make with these alternatives; it's a death grip. Our inner lives become like my great-uncle's house, cluttered and choked with so much paraphernalia that it is impossible to see clearly or live freely. To maneuver past this second landmark means something more than a little spring cleaning. It requires a complete renovation. For we have all become hoarders. We have all trashed our hearts. We have all given ourselves over to idols.

> For we have all become hoarders. We have all trashed our hearts. We have all given ourselves over to idols.

Idolatry as an Exchange

In today's vernacular, we generally don't use the term *idol*. Instead, we call it an *addiction*, but the basic meaning is the same. An idol, or addiction, is simply a substitution tactic. We may think that it's no different than exchanging the wrong size shirt for the right one, but this is no casual swap. We are attempting to replace God's captivating presence for something of far lesser value. The Bible puts it this way: "They became fools and . . . exchanged the truth of God for a lie, and worshiped and served something created instead of the Creator" (Rom. 1:22, 25).

Think of your favorite author—perhaps Austen or Dickens or Steinbeck—and then imagine an evening where you are reading one of their books as you sit by a warm, crackling fire. The doorbell rings and you answer. Wonder of wonders, it is the very same author at the door, wanting to come in for a chat. And guess what about? The very book you are reading! Your response to such a momentous invitation? "I'm really sorry, but I am too busy reading your book to spend time with you." What would we say to such a reply? "You fool! How could you be so blind? Couldn't you have let the author in for the evening and then spent the next night reading his book with a whole new appreciation?"

This is the tragedy of idolatry. We are all that foolish. We are all at some level convinced that the real deal is not found with God, so we run to what He has created. The idiocy of the exchange is further heightened by what it does to us. Just like the ring, idols corrupt. Rather than our hearts being mirrors reflecting the radiant glory of God, they become enslaved, then darkened, and finally hardened. So why in the world would anyone give themselves to idols? What's the draw? What's the allure?

> We are all at some level convinced that the real deal is not found with God, so we run to what He has created.

The universal appeal of idolatry lies in the mirage it presents. Idols enchant us with the illusion that we can maintain control and manage pain.

Here is our dilemma at present. We can't see God or touch Him. Worse yet, we can't control Him. To rely on Him to be our life, our provision, our happiness appears too unpredictable. So it seems perfectly reasonable to look to idols. Now instead of dealing with an unknown commodity like God, idols seem not only controllable but tangible as well. We can get our hands on them. In addition, idols appear to soothe our ache for happiness, certainly a competitive offer with what we may have heard about God. But idols sweeten the deal with a compelling incentive—relief from pain. It seems that God doesn't do that for us. Or perhaps He can't. Otherwise, why are our lives marked with sadness and difficulty? Finally, there is one last selling point: the type of relief idols offer is immediate. God might come through in the end, or He might not, but we're not going to wait around to find out. Who wants the agony of post-op pain when the nurse is offering morphine? With such thinking, the leap into idolatry seems perfectly justifiable.

There is a tragic footnote to this exchange. We are not simply running *to* an idol, we are also running *from* God. This is not just a theological problem or a psychological issue. This is personal rejection. God's anger in the Bible has been widely misunderstood. It is not the wrath of an overbearing tyrant, but the anger of a jilted lover. It is the anger of a husband betrayed by his wife. And behind the anger is hurt. And behind the hurt is grief. It is worth pausing to consider that at the center of all reality is a broken heart, and it's not ours. Idolatry is a rejection of the living God who wants to father us, cherish us, and delight in us. But we run away and wound Him in the process.

> It is worth pausing to consider that at the center of all reality is a broken heart, and it's not ours.

Stories of Idolatry

We tend to put idols in the category of disreputable habits, such as alcoholism or sexual addiction or anorexia. But idols can appear perfectly respectable. In fact, we can be praised for them. My own story is a case study in this. Take this example from my early years as a youth minister.

The Easter service was unusually crowded at the suburban church where I worked. The preaching and music had been uplifting, and people lingered in conversation long after the service was over. Finally, everyone slowly trickled away to family dinners or picnics. But where did I go? To my office. To do what? Sort papers into my elaborate filing system.

If I had been by myself, I wouldn't have thought much about it. But being newly married, Heidi was with me. I asked her to come, promising her it wouldn't take long. An hour later, I had worked through the stacks of paper and mail and meticulously found the right spot for each. There was a sense of satisfaction about getting my desk in order for the next day. But Heidi didn't feel that way; she just felt confused. Why did I feel the need to file on Easter Sunday? Why didn't I join in some church gathering or initiate one myself? After all, I was a minister. As I look back, it really wasn't a choice; it was a necessity. I had to go and file. I was a slave. I was addicted to order.

This wasn't just about my filing system; it was the way I handled all of life. My shirts had to be lined up by color. The rugs had to be vacuumed. The car had to be spotless. Very few items held sentimental value. If they weren't functional, they were tossed in the trash. I had my lists of projects, lists of things to do for the day, lists of books to read, lists of goals for the year, lists of people to call. I even had a list of my lists. Maybe you think I was as disturbed as my great-uncle. Maybe you're right. But that's not how others perceived me. I was seen as incredibly disciplined and self-motivated, and I was stroked for it. But deep down inside I knew there was something wrong, and I had no idea how to get out of it. I was chained to a way of life that I had used for years to handle my internal messiness. It was my morphine, my ring. That momentary sense of accomplishment was just enough to keep the loneliness and depression at bay and to keep me feeling in control. I felt no heart connection to others in a way that would allow me to desire their company. Sure, I was efficient. But loving God and others is not a matter of efficiency. It's a matter of the heart. And I had lost mine a long time ago. Or perhaps it's truer to say that I had sold it into slavery.

This pattern of compulsion extended from my childhood on into my later adult years. Each new fixation became an attempt to shock my heart back to life. There was the stamp-collecting craze as a preteen and the flirtation with pornography as a teenager. Next I began to hoard clothes and clutch at possessions, like

> But loving God and others is not a matter of effeciency. It's a matter of the heart.

my car (shades of my great-uncle perhaps). Then, in college, came the discovery of running. I found myself running more and more so that I could eat enormous amounts of food for dinner as the prize. That kept my growing depression manageable. But of course it also set me up to repeat the cycle the next day. Running was no longer fun; it was a necessity. I had to run each day. I have already mentioned my obsession with being a successful teacher and coach. Failure there was just not an option. And the list went on and on, an endless string of idols, all of them seducing me, crippling me, and crushing me. My heart was so badly mangled that I wonder how I survived. I was breathing, but that's about all.

As I have since listened to the stories of many others, I have found my experience paralleled in theirs. The idols can be respectable ones like many of mine were, or they can be the more disreputable kind. It doesn't really matter, for the energy behind them is the same—control and pain management.

I have a dear friend who was born out of wedlock. His parents treated him as the mistake they never wanted. There was never any important conversation, any affirmation, any encouragement. Once, as a teenager, he asked his father for advice concerning a painful dating situation he found himself in. His father responded with a blank stare and walked away. So to fill the aching void of disconnection, he turned to idols. He became successful as a football player and was admired for his athletic ability. But it was no longer a game. Each contest became a life-or-death matter. To overcome his fear of others, he turned to alcohol, only to find it becoming a necessary crutch for social engagement. And to sedate that terrible sense of being unwanted, he hooked himself to girlfriends, to academic success, to food, to anything that would give him relief. But in the end all his addictions began to corrupt him, and his fear resurfaced to cripple him. That's always what happens with idols. They offer us the illusion of mastery, but like Tolkien's ring, they master us instead, and we are left worse off than before.

Letting Go of Idols

Letting go of our idols has a price tag, for it is a descent into the unknown. That's what this second landmark is all about. Often the unknown consists of all the unfelt pain and sadness we have avoided. Our idols have functioned as emotional junk food to give us a quick high. But now we find that we must fast from them, and the prospect of doing so is unsettling. *What will I do without it?* Imagine being a five-year-old and told that you must part with your beloved teddy bear forever. That's the feel. It's a death to something we have used for comfort and support.

Yet we are ready to face this, for now we recognize the mirage that our idols have been. Instead of helping us, they have hurt us deeply. We see the deception we have swallowed. We hate what we have become. We want to change and are ready for God.

The first time I ever rappelled was off of a sixty-foot cliff. As I shuffled toward the edge, I remember feeling queasy with anxiety. When the moment of commitment came, I had to lean backward, step off the cliff, and trust that the rope would hold me. The first several feet were terrifying, but my fear gradually turned into confidence as I inched my way downward. By the time I reached the bottom I was so exhilarated that I wanted to do it again. Something similar happens when we detach ourselves from idols and attach to the living God. We give up the controllable for the unmanageable, the familiar for the unknown. God tells us to rely on Him, but we can't restrict Him. We simply have to step off and believe He will hold us. Only then can we begin to feel the life He offers.

Depending on the particular idol or brand of addiction, the actual letting go will look different. In some cases, like substance abuse or pornography, we just need to stop. Period. Whatever it takes, whatever it costs, whatever help is needed from others. But cutting off other idols is trickier. It becomes a matter of limiting and looking to God in the moment. You may need to reduce your time at work, or your time at the mall, or your time watching television. My

> God tells us to rely on Him, but we can't restrict Him. We simply have to step off and believe He will hold us.

compulsion with exercise and food fits here. I obviously needed to keep eating, and exercise was still good, but I had to make all sorts of lifestyle changes and then ask God to help me keep attuned to Him instead of zoning out with my old idol.

God as the Surgeon

But with most of our idols, we soon discover that doing our part isn't enough. Sometimes a vine can entwine itself around a small tree so tightly that it appears the only way to kill the vine is to kill the tree. It can feel that way with our idols. They wrap themselves around our hearts so that extricating ourselves can feel hopeless. In *Lord of the Rings*, Frodo has every good intention of taking the ring and destroying it by casting it back into the fires of Mt. Doom. He does his part by making it to the mountain. That's the whole quest. But at the climactic moment, he can't do it. He can't let it go. The ring has taken hold of him.

Detaching an idol from our heart can seem like removing our own appendix. We know it has to come out. But where do we cut? How deep do we cut? Defeated, we throw down the scalpel. We can't do this on our own. It's then we realize that God has to do the surgery. He has to remove our idols. Our part is to get on the operating table and let Him cut, however He chooses.

What does it mean to let go and let God be the surgeon? What does it look like? It often happens in the daily stuff of life. Something happens, something is said, something is done to trigger the desire or surface the pain. Instead of running to our idol, we stop and allow ourselves to stay empty, to stay aching. We refuse to go back, no matter how much the desire pulls at us, no matter how much the pain screams at us. It is the emotional equivalent of going through cocaine withdrawal.

> It's then we realize that God has to do the surgery. He has to remove our idols.

This is where the truth from Isaiah 50 offers so much hope:

> Who among you walks in darkness, and has no light? Let him trust in the name of Yahweh; let him lean on his God. Look, all you who kindle a fire, who encircle yourselves with firebrands; walk in the light of your fire and in the firebrands you have lit! This is what you'll get from My hand: you will lie down in a place of torment. (vv. 10–11)

When we find ourselves in the darkness with no apparent relief in sight, we are asked to rely on God, to hang our heart's desire on Him. The other option is to go back to our idols and keep managing life by lighting our own fires. But the result is heartbreaking; there is no relief, only more torment. So we choose to wait in the darkness and hope that God will come through. And here our fear deepens: *How will God come through? When will He come through? What if He doesn't? What will I do?* But we know there's no going back. So we wait.

Yet even with the sure promise of His help, there is no formula for how it will come. Remember, we are told to rely on Him, but we can't restrict Him. Sometimes God will make a truth from Scripture come alive with such power that it feels like a hot scalpel, cutting the idol out. Sometimes He will send the encouragement of friends who know our hearts and can speak into our lives. Sometimes He will deliver insight through a wise counselor. Sometimes God will speak personally to our hearts with something we need to hear or do. And sometimes He will just come and transform us in a way beyond our ability to explain or describe.

> When we find ourselves in the darkness with no apparent relief in sight, we are asked to rely on God, to hang our heart's desire on Him.

How long will it take? Again, there is no formula. There will be moments when God shifts things in our hearts in a felt way. Sometimes this will happen in one climactic moment, sometimes in multiple ones, before an idol no longer grips us. At other times, there will be a very gradual change that we hardly notice. But the result will be the same: we will find ourselves having crossed a bridge into another land that we once saw only from a distance.

A Brief Narrative of Letting Go

I mentioned my drivenness with coaching in the previous landmark. Here is the rest of that story.

On the day track season officially began, Heidi often felt like wearing black because she was going into mourning. For the next three months, I was basically nonexistent at home. I had a state-ranked team that needed training and preparation. I had a reputation to keep up, and that meant more time, more work, and more preparation. I also needed larger teams to ensure more victories to keep placing high in the state. And larger teams meant even more time, more work, and more preparation. I think you see where all this is going. On the outside, I looked like a successful coach. But that's not what I felt on the inside. I felt pressure and fear, driven to succeed because that was where I found the affirmation I had failed to find in high school. In short, coaching track had become my identity. There was simply no way I could ever think about stopping.

But after eight years of nearly round-the-clock coaching, I was drained, empty, and exhausted. My ring was corrupting me. On top of that, Heidi and the girls were suffering from my absence. My teaching was also suffering. I knew I had to stop. I struggled with the decision, but after a conversation with my assistant coach, I found the courage to resign. At the time it felt like I was cutting off my own arm, but soon after there was a tremendous sense of relief and freedom. I had done my part in letting go, but a deeper work still needed to be done in my heart.

A few years later, I attended the regional finals at a track where I had spent much time during my coaching career. I knew some students who were competing, and I wanted to be there to cheer them on. I entered the stadium and went immediately to the infield. The runners and coaches were all milling around, talking about strategy, encouraging each other, or just socializing. As I began to converse with some of the runners, pleasant memories of past meets edged in on my consciousness. I loved being out there in the middle of all the action again, thinking about all the races I had coached there.

> I had done my part in letting go, but a deeper work still needed to be done in my heart.

But in the midst of it, I began to sense something that I can only describe as a prickling. It's what an alcoholic may feel when he looks at a bottle after being sober for years and wonders what a drink would taste like. As I left the infield and returned to the stands to cheer, I felt a massive pull to return to coaching track. Outwardly, I was having a great time sitting with a couple of close buddies, but inwardly, I was being wrenched by old hooks. Sure, I had quit coaching several years ago, but a deeper work was about to happen that I did not yet understand. All I knew was that the power of the lure was increasing and my restlessness and pain were mounting. I felt trapped in a familiar haunt I thought I had left.

With the track meet almost over, I decided to leave. I got into my truck and began the ride home, upset and unsettled. Tears of sadness flowed at leaving behind something that had meant so much to me. Then I realized what I needed to do: I needed to wait in the darkness and trust the Father to come through. And then the revelation came.

This is how I think it happens so many times. When we choose to wait, the Father helps us see something new about our hearts. I realized at that moment that what I was seeking in coaching was not only connection, but also validation. I had hoped that my success as a coach would prove to myself and to the world that I was a man. There is nothing wrong with the longing to be called out as a man, but that longing had been crushed many years earlier and then reawakened when I began to coach track. I then hooked the longing to coaching in a desperate attempt to find value as a man. But whatever you trust to validate you can also invalidate you; hence, all the fear, the striving, and the exhaustion that had been underneath so much of my coaching. I could not fail because I feared being exposed as a weak and pitiful boy with nothing to offer but my own ineptness.

> Whatever you trust to validate you can also invalidate you.

I then understood as never before why I had coached track all those years, and I realized that track could never validate me. Only my Father could do that. I am His son, His beloved son, His cherished son. He can call me out as a man, and He was doing it right there on the truck ride home. The tears of sadness turned into tears of wonder. The ring was being cut off. I found myself having crossed a bridge into a territory I had only seen from a distance. And now I was there, ready to push ahead.

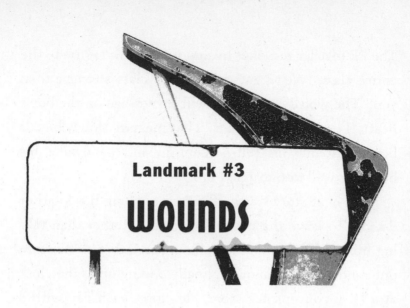

Landmark #3

WOUNDS

To be alive at all is to have scars.

—JOHN STEINBECK

In my deepest wound I saw Your glory, and it dazzled me.

—AUGUSTINE

We live among the walking wounded. We breathe their air, eat their food, and hear their cries. For they are us. I have heard many of their stories. Here are three.

The first one begins in the sixth grade with a scrawny, unsure boy who has not yet reached puberty. It is PE class, and the day is given over to fitness tests. He approaches the pull-up bar with anxiety. Giving it his best shot, his worst fear becomes reality. He can't do even one pull-up.

The PE teacher responds by announcing his failure to the entire class: "We've got girls in this class stronger than you." The words carve an indelible message on the boy's heart: "I can never be a man." That message slowly bleeds him, poisoning his self-perception and paralyzing his behavior well into married life.

The next story starts off when a young boy's father decides to leave the pastoral ministry. Rather than taking up another honorable calling, the father shifts from one random job to another, finally ending up as the clerk at a local convenience store. He closes each day with a half bottle of whiskey. For the son, life at home becomes the miserable chore of trying to appease a drunken dad who explodes in tirades of rage. The boy lives in constant dread. What is he supposed to do? What is he to believe about himself? What is he to believe about God?

The final story opens in a third-grade classroom. The teacher is a sour, elderly woman who should have retired long ago. One day in class she asks a boy to read aloud. Not being the best of readers, he hesitates, stalls, and stutters on certain words. The teacher finally interrupts, "You are so stupid!" Those four words will become his identity for the next ten years until his sophomore year of college. There, after finally making good grades, it occurs to him that his third-grade teacher might have been wrong. Maybe he isn't so dumb after all.

I happen to know these stories well because they belong to three of my close colleagues, good men whose sadness you would not suspect if you met them today. Though their stories are certainly sorrowful, there are others out there far worse. But what strikes me in all this is how universal they are. Underneath everyone's exterior lies enough anguish to tempt even the cynical to weep.

This is the landscape of the third landmark, a descent into the wounds that have been inflicted on us. And *descent* is the proper term here, for our first reaction is to bury them, deep into the basement of our souls. We never want to talk about them. We never want to think about them.

> Underneath everyone's exterior lies enough anguish to tempt even the cynical to weep.

Probing the Wound

The commitment to hiding our wounds is of course understandable. At least with our idols, we know who the offender is even if we can't stop. It's our own doing, our own problem. But when it comes to our wounds, we confront a new level of terror. None of this was in our control. None of this was our doing. And the terror provokes unsettling questions. What kind of world do we live in where wounding is the norm? What kind of God allows this type of thing to happen as a matter of general course? And when our questions get returned with silence, the terror grows. Maybe we really are alone in the world. If God isn't going to do anything, we've got to. So we hunt, scrape, scour for something to comfort us, anything to ease the agony.

Here lies the hidden connection to idols. For idols not only highlight our commitment to exchange the Creator for the created, they also point out how we have handled our wounds. Long after we see the devastation an idol has produced in our lives, we can still cling to it precisely because it promises relief. But once we begin to release our grip on it, it will lead us into the wound. All of the submerged pain will rise to the surface, like a beach ball forced underwater that is finally let loose. Jesus Himself connected the two landmarks: "Forgive us our sins as we forgive those who sin against us" (Matt. 6:12 NIV). Once we take in the forgiveness God offers us for our idols, we are now obligated to deal with the wounds others have dealt us.

As a boy, I was fascinated with the demolition car derbies I watched on TV. Cars would recklessly speed around an open field trying to knock each other out. As the derby went on, there was an increasing jungle of stalled vehicles often crushed into unrecognizable forms. The last car moving was declared the winner. That's a pretty good visual for life, a chaotic tangle of people smashing into each other. For we do not exist as disconnected individuals, fallen only because of our self-inflicted idolatry. Everything is not our fault. We also live out of our fallen family lineages and out of countless collisions that have impacted us. Not only is our own car broken, but other cars keep smashing into it.

> Once we take in the forgiveness God offers us for our idols, we are now obligated to deal with the wounds others have dealt us.

Realizing this is just a halting step toward this landmark; the real journey is still ahead and still very much unknown. It is a descent into the pain that we have shellacked over with our idols, our personality, our theology, anything to keep it at bay. Now we are being asked to enter in. Do we really want to do this? *Can* we do this?

Owning

The first step forward, if we're ready, is to simply own the wound, to admit that it happened, to admit that it hurt. At first you may think this wouldn't be so difficult, but remember, our impulse is to hide it, dismiss it. We can take the evil inflicted on us and casually wave it off. *It's not that big of a deal. I'm okay. Worse things have happened to others.* We may think this is having a positive attitude, but it's a sham. I have listened to others relate the terrible abandonment they have felt from their parents and then in the very next breath excuse it—"It was the best they could do. They didn't know any better." It's offered in the name of love and forgiveness, but it's neither. It's excuse-making of the highest order. If we dismiss our wounds, we don't have to feel it. This is the route of straight denial.

Another one of my colleagues is a wonderful woman of grace and compassion, but her story is plagued by thirty years of disconnection and denial. As a young girl of six, she remembers walking home from school one day in the snow, happy and carefree, wearing her new red boots. When she reached her street, an anxious neighbor greeted her and called her inside, keeping her from walking on to her own home. The girl sensed something was terribly wrong, and then saw an ambulance in her driveway. Later that afternoon, she was told that her father had been rushed to the hospital. He was soon diagnosed with brain cancer, and three years later she lost him to that terrible disease.

How was she to respond? What was she to feel? Without anyone telling her, she decided that she had to be strong for everyone else. This was her way of disconnecting from the sadness. And it fit right in with her family's pattern, where strong women were prized and affirmed. But there was a huge price tag for this maneuver; she became emotionally dishonest. On the surface she told everyone she was fine, but underneath she was stalked by anger, especially at things she couldn't control. The rage eventually boiled over at her adolescent son whom she could not manage. Interestingly, it was his anger and erratic behavior that brought her to the breaking point. Seeing her anger reflected in his broke her heart. She was going to have to reconnect to the sadness. She was going to have to face her father's death.

This is what so often happens when we refuse to admit the wound. We are convinced that owning it would kill us, but it is running away that kills us. This pattern of avoidance is so contrary to how pain is approached in the Bible. Take the Psalms for instance. Although ordinarily thought of as songs of praise, there is so much more to them. In fact, the praise psalm is not even the most common type. That distinction belongs to the lament psalm, a song of grief and sadness. Time after time, we find the writers of the lament psalms owning their anguish with piercing honesty. There is not a whiff of denial or excuse at the injustice they feel. Instead, they wrestle with God: "My whole being is shaken with terror. And You, O LORD—how long?" (Ps. 6:3).

> We are convinced that owning it would kill us, but it is running away that kills us.

"LORD, why do You stand so far away? Why do You hide in times of trouble?" (Ps. 10:1). "I will say to God, my rock, 'Why have You forgotten me? Why must I go about in sorrow because the enemy's oppression?'" (Ps. 42:9).

Each of these psalms starts in agony but ends in worship. Somehow as the writers grappled with their sorrow, they found God. It should strike us as odd as it is surprising that running away from our wounds may be running away from God.

> It should strike us as odd as it is surprising that running away from our wounds may be running away from God.

Maybe owning them is how we find Him. Maybe the wound is His call to come and wrestle with Him.

With that new thought, we decide to take a further step toward this landmark. But now we come to a cliff where we see our next step. It's a leap. We are being asked to grieve.

Grieving

My colleague who lost her father said that when she began to grieve, she feared it would never end, that she would never stop crying. For three tumultuous days she lay in her bed, weeping, unable to get up, while her children tenderly waited on her. She wrestled with God over her loss. *Where was God? Why did this happen?* It sounds so much like the lament psalms.

My own story with grief parallels hers. For twenty years I kept running away from the wounds of my early life. Through God's cunning providence, I found myself in my mid-thirties accepting a position to teach high school after I had left the pastoral ministry. Without my permission or even my understanding, I was taken back to the place where so much of the wounding had begun.

I could no longer run. I was being asked to grieve.

My first experience of this was messy. It was the beginning of my second year at the school, and I was talking with some of the football players after practice about the newly instituted football program. As the conversation progressed, I suddenly felt something disturbing awaken inside of me. The grief was starting to surface, and football as the trigger, arousing old feelings of disconnection and sadness. I had always wanted to play the sport and be on the team, but I had been too scared to try at the time. As I continued to talk to the players, I felt the agitation increase until I finally had to leave so I could be alone. I walked toward a deserted field in the back of the property. I didn't know what was happening, but just let the sadness come up. It was as if I had tapped into a pressurized pool of lava. What came up was a volcano of emotion. I found myself sobbing uncontrollably. I was starting to grieve.

Lamentations is the Bible's storybook of grief. In it, Jeremiah the prophet chronicles the capture of Jerusalem in horrific detail—the siege by the Babylonians, the burning of the city, the destruction of the temple, the terrible famine, and the anguish of the people. His description is structured in such a way to give full vent to his grief. Each chapter of the book, except the last one, is an acrostic poem in which every letter of the Hebrew alphabet is used to begin a new line (as we might write a poem that begins with the letter A, the next line with the letter B, and so on). All the pain, from A to Z, is recorded just as it was experienced. Nothing is left out or denied.

I am struck by how different Jeremiah's approach is to our usual avoidance of grief. I think if he were alive today, we would accuse him of being morose. We would probably tell him to lighten up and look on the bright side. But Jeremiah is insistent on giving grief its voice. And the payoff is profound. He finds God.

Sometimes in Hebrew verse the most important point is put right in the center of the poem. It is just so here. In the very middle of the book of Lamentations, where the darkness is deepest, erupts one of the most poignant statements about God's love in the entire Bible:

> Because of the LORD's great love we are not consumed, for his compassions never fail. They are new every morning; great is your faithfulness! (Lam. 3:22–23 NIV)

We often try to own this truth without the surrounding context of darkness and grief in the rest of the book. We try to circumvent the process, pasting the idea on top of our wounds as another avoidance mechanism. But it doesn't work. We haven't yet grieved the wound.

Walking through this landmark, I have had to grieve so many things, both what was lost and what should never have been. I have had to revisit my wounds one by one, from A to Z. There was the loss of any substantive connection to my parents at an early age, the absence of any man to guide me or speak into my life, the first love that ended in heartbreak, the lack of bonding with my peers, the intellectual darkness as I drifted into atheism and pantheism, and the loss of so much of my life to twenty years of depression. But as I have wandered through the sadness, the confusion, and at times the rage, I am no longer just jabbering about the love of God. I feel it. I know it.

And this is where grief takes us. It's not something to just slog through and endure. Instead, grief becomes the suture that begins to close the terrible chasm between our head and our heart. When we grieve, we simply allow our hearts to speak to us about what really happened instead of intellectualizing it or excusing it. As we do this, grief transforms the deep structures of our hearts. For

> Instead, grief becomes the suture that begins to close the terrible chasm between our head and our heart.

the way we deal with life is so often some form of protection against pain. It soon crystallizes in order to survive the onslaught. And over time the structure hardens like steel. But allowing our sadness to flow over into tears begins the melting. Our hearts come alive again, sometimes searing with desire, but alive nonetheless.

Grief also helps us clarify what our hearts truly long for. The idols that once pulled at us no longer seem to have the same draw. They are emptied of power because we now know they aren't what we long for. What we truly ache for is a Father who will come to us with compassions that are new every morning. And He does come. Jesus Himself said that our mourning would be blessed because there we will find comfort (Matt. 5:4). It is the comfort of one who sympathizes, for Jesus Himself was a man of sorrows and acquainted with grief (Isa. 53:3).

Forgiving

There is a final challenge in rounding this landmark: the tricky maneuver of forgiving. As mentioned earlier, we can often confuse forgiving the offender with excusing the offense. Yet these are two very different responses. Excusing implies that the wound didn't really hurt, that it really didn't matter. But forgiveness requires drinking the whole offense down to its bitter dregs and then refusing to hold it against the offender.

Think about how God deals with us. He certainly doesn't excuse our idols. He doesn't pretend that we haven't wounded Him with our betrayal. Instead, He chooses to feel the weight of the offense, the sadness, the anger, the loss. Much of the Old Testament is a journal of God's struggle with the treachery of His people. His response culminates in the New Testament where His Son took on the weight of all our idolatry, bearing it on His shoulders until it crushed Him. Only then does He extend forgiveness. If God simply excused us, then the torture and death of His Son was a colossal waste.

> Forgiveness requires drinking the whole offense down to its bitter dregs and then refusing to hold it against the offender.

Even so, this doesn't answer all the questions we may have about our own wounding. Some answers may come in time; others may remain hidden forever. But what this does point out is the path we should take. It is to own our wounds, grieve them, and then forgive where we need to.

As previously mentioned, Jesus Himself taught us to pray, "Forgive us our debts, as we also have forgiven our debtors" (Matt. 6:12). He was implying that our ability to feel the forgiveness of the Father is dependent upon our forgiveness of others. As we let go of what others have done to us, there is a place opened in our hearts that was once sealed off. Forgiveness isn't really about setting the offender free; it's about setting ourselves free.

However, understanding Jesus' words in no way lessens the risks involved in forgiving or the questions we may face in the process. *Does forgiving mean I have to somehow forget the offense? Is there a right time to confront the offender? What exactly do I say to the person who has harmed me? Is forgiving just a one-time experience? What if the person denies what he has done? What if he hurts me again? And what about those whom I have harmed? Don't I need to go and ask their forgiveness?* These and other questions may come up as we descend into the unknown territory of forgiveness. But rather than trying to answer every question, perhaps a story would be more helpful.

My father grew up in an era when being a good father meant being the provider for the family. As such, he did his job well as a doctor. I was one of five children and, being compliant and quiet, gave the impression that I didn't need much attention. Combine this with my father's busy schedule, and I can recall only fragments of any real interaction. There was just a void. My father was also a very anxious person, both because of the stress of his work and the stress of his inner world. He was prone to sudden outbreaks of anger, and from an early age I remember being afraid of them. Once, while trying to put together stereo speakers for the den, he got frustrated and then irate. I was trying to help him and felt that it was somehow my responsibility to find a way to calm him down. In that moment I felt a separation, a wall going up that kept him out and protected me. I had already become comfortable living in my own private world as a child. Perhaps I really didn't need a father after all.

The wall only grew thicker in adolescence as I began to act out my independence. It's not that I thought about asking my father for help or advice and then rejected the idea. It simply never occurred to me to ask him. Once, when trying to put on a rented tux, I struggled to put on the cuff links and cummerbund. I then went on to the formal date without the bow tie because I couldn't find it tucked away in the packaging. The shame at not being dressed properly gnawed at me for the entire evening. Yet while getting ready, I never once thought about asking my father for help. I just assumed that I was on my own to figure it out.

While in seminary, one of my close friends observed, "You know, the thing about you, Bill, is that you don't really need anyone." I had convinced everyone of this, including myself. But it was a lie. I really needed others, and I especially needed a father. So many things would have been different with a father's encouragement and presence; so much darkness would have been avoided.

When I began to walk through the process of grieving, I realized I had to stop running away from my father.

I had to face the abandonment and quit excusing it. I remember on one particular day the anger toward him surfaced while I was driving. The rage came out as I pounded my fists on the steering wheel. It frightened me to see what I had locked up inside.

Sometime later came the terrifying moment when I actually confronted my father. He needed to know what I felt; otherwise, there could be no hope of real relationship. I was so nervous that I had to write out what I was going to say and then read it to him. His response surprised me. There was little defensiveness and no hostility, just sadness and an expressed desire to change. Something moved inside my heart, compassion tinged with hope. The wall was starting to come down.

Then the day came when I decided to get my father to talk about his father, something he rarely did. We were enjoying coffee in a local shop, and I simply asked, "Dad, what did you do with your father while you were growing up?" I will never forget his response. He looked down and said nothing for about ten seconds. When he finally lifted his head and looked at me, he responded in a downcast tone, "Well, that about says it, doesn't it?" It all clicked. I understood. He was just handing down what had been handed to him. I began to see my own father not as an enemy, but as a fatherless man himself. The wall was crumbling. That feeling only deepened when I inquired about my great-grandfather in a later conversation. My father informed me that the only thing he ever heard his father say about him was that he was a very quiet man.

So I am the fourth generation of men disconnected from their fathers. It is my fallen lineage. But it can stop now. Forgiveness has made it possible.

During a recent Thanksgiving, I ended up being alone with my father for dinner at his retirement home. He asked me to pray for the meal, and then reached his hand toward mine, wanting me to hold it. I felt something like electricity arc between us. Whatever I said in the prayer was not nearly as important as what was unsaid. My father was expressing that he wanted connection, and my heart was finally free to offer it. In that moment, the darkness, the confusion, the sadness, all of it faded. The struggle to get to this landmark had been so worth it. But more lay ahead.

Landmark #4

SEX

. The first two facts which a healthy boy or girl feels
about sex are these: first that it is beautiful
and then that it is dangerous.

—G. K. CHESTERTON

Nobody dies from the lack of sex. It's lack of love we die from.

—MARGARET ATWOOD

Rummaging through some of my memories while writing one day, I ran across several that jarred me with their strangeness and sadness.

In the first one, I was standing in the lobby of an auto repair shop, waiting for my car to be fixed. I forgot to bring a book to read, so I rummaged through the magazine rack situated next to a droning television. I eventually found a catalog that caught my attention, one filled with various buses for sale. I flipped through it simply because I'd never seen such a catalog before. I stopped at a two-page ad for a deluxe model bus. Standing next to it was a scantily clad woman holding her arms as if she were pointing to the grand prize on a game show. I wondered, *What is a half-naked woman doing in a bus catalog?* And then it hit me. I knew why. So I would stop and look.

The next memory was of a New Year's Day gathering Heidi and I attended at the home of some friends. As people were milling about, I struck up a conversation with a man whom I had respected for some time as a teacher and counselor. As our discussion shifted from surface pleasantries to men and their struggles, he told me about the growing number of men he was counseling who were out of control sexually. Some were frequenting prostitutes while others were living double lives, with a wife at home and a homosexual lover hidden away. He then stunned me with his next comment. Many of these men were leaders in their churches.

The high school where I taught was the setting of the next memory. Two women, both college professors, gave a presentation to some of the student body about sexual behavior in college. The students were drawn in by their honesty and expertise. While they were speaking, they began to share personally about their own motivation for coming to class that day: they were burdened by the disturbing trends they had seen in the collegiate women who came to them for counseling. Some of these women were unaware of the STDs they were infected with, while others had fallen victim to date rape drugs, and still more had suffered all kinds of sexual abuse. I shuddered and then felt a twinge of anger. I have two daughters.

Another memory occurred in the same school, but this time it was a classroom of young men. In this particular class, I had various men come as guests throughout the semester and tell their stories. Some were faculty, some were coaches, and others were parents. On one particular day I had invited a close friend who was also a pastor. As he shared his story, he took the risk to tell how he had used women sexually in college to cover his own insecurity and how he felt regret over this actions. The young men were appreciative of his honesty, and so was I. Then it struck me: almost every man invited to address this class had shared some brand of sexual brokenness, all without my prompting. It seemed no one was exempt.

The final memory was also from that school. One of the men I had once worked with in youth ministry years before approached me in the hallway with troubling news. He told me the tragic story of a youth minister who had been convicted on multiple counts of sexual assault. It seems that this minister had taken young men on camping trips, drugged them, and then sexually abused them. After his conviction, he was imprisoned for life only to be found dead one morning from an epileptic seizure. The story sickened me, even without hearing all of the details. But what horrified me was that he was no stranger; my friend and I both knew him. He had once worked with us in ministry before this behavior began.

All of us have memories like these that both haunt us and repel us. It is these types of stories that trace the terrain of the fourth landmark, one not just of sexual brokenness and confusion, but one of sexual insanity.

In some ways this landmark covers the same type of terrain we have already navigated through with idols and wounds, for sex may be the most seductive of all idols. And it can play a role in the wounds we receive. But as we approach this landmark, everything becomes even tighter, tenser than before. It's a further descent into a jungle filled with land mines of guilt and shame. We want to come out alive. But how? How do we ever find a way out?

Going Insane

The idols landmark pointed out the foolishness of exchanging our connection to the Author of life with an obsession over His creation. We think this is a good idea only because the insanity of our fallenness has already begun to work its spell on us: "Claiming to be wise, they became fools" (Rom. 1:22). But with sex, the exchange becomes more acute, as does the insanity: "Therefore

God delivered them over in the cravings of their hearts to sexual impurity, so that their bodies were degraded among themselves" (v. 24). The degradation described in the next several verses spirals out of control, from the heterosexual into the homosexual. Only after the sexual corruption has played itself out does the rest of our sadness appear in the lineup: "They are filled with all unrighteousness, evil, greed, and wickedness. They are full of envy, murder, quarrels, deceit, and malice" (v. 29).

It's as if the fall of man is a massive earthquake, and the epicenter appears to be sex. Something so precious is being demolished. It's like taking the Louvre art collection in Paris and setting it on fire. It's insane.

At its core, sexual immorality is a substitution of the invisible God for the visible, naked human body. The reason this exchange is so alluring is that sex embodies so much of what real communion with God is supposed to feel like—connection, pleasure, intimacy. What we feel during orgasm is a backward glance at Eden, a heightened sense of joy with a momentary loss of self-consciousness and shame. Or, if we look forward, it reveals a glimpse of heaven.

> At its core, sexual immorality is a substitution of the invisible God for the visible, naked human body.

But if sex is so wonderful, why is it so damaging? The answer lies in the question itself. Sex is so destructive *precisely because it is so good*. The same is true of many things in life. The greater the power something has for good, the greater its potential for evil. Fire can save you from frostbite and purify gold. It can also destroy your house and inflict horrendous pain. And our sexual insanity here is playing with fire.

A Strange Response

God's response to our sexual insanity appears at first to be as strange as the insanity itself. It is described as we look again at Romans 1:24: "Therefore God delivered them over. . . ." This simple phrase is repeated two more times for emphasis in the same passage. We normally think of God's response to immorality and foolishness as one of judgment and wrath. But here He just gives us over to our idolatry. It may sound like God is indifferent, as if He really doesn't care all that much about us in the first place, and now He's relieved to finally be rid of us. Imagine a boss who never really liked a certain employee and has just been waiting for that employee to make enough mistakes so that he has good reason to fire him. God's response seems to feel like that.

But I think a truer parallel may be the father in the parable of the prodigal son. The son comes to him one day with an unusual request: "Father, give me the share of the estate I have coming to me" (Luke 15:12). The implied insult is brutal, for the son is essentially saying, "As far as I am concerned, Father, you're dead already. I don't want anything to do with you. Give me what's mine so I don't have to wait around for you to die." The father's response is just as shocking: "So he distributed the assets to them" (v. 12). There is no argument, no angry outburst; the father just complies. He gives his son over to what he asked for and lets him go. The crushing sadness behind such a response is not hard to imagine.

Perhaps then God gives us over to our sexual idols in somewhat the same way. It's not that He no longer cares about us. It's that in giving us this terrible permission, we may come to understand the truth. Our idols are not what we want after all. What we really want is a father. And that's exactly what happens to the rebellious son. He spends all his inheritance on the party lifestyle until, starving one day, he finds himself eyeing pig slop. This is not what he wants anymore. He's had enough. He wants to go home.

All of our sexual insanity then, whether premarital or extramarital sex, pornography, same-sex attraction, bisexuality, or masturbation, is not really about sex at all. Underneath it all lies a compulsion of the heart, a yearning to connect to a Father. It's an ache that will never go away no matter how much we ignore it or push it down. And it will never be satisfied with whatever sexual habit we have used to manage the longing.

> Underneath it all lies a compulsion of the heart, a yearning to connect to a Father. It's an ache that will never go away no matter how much we ignore it or push it down.

We come now to the same place we reached with the landmark of idols. If the fall of man was the irrational exchange of the living God for lifeless idols, then our healing comes through a reverse motion, by returning to the Father through Jesus. We will not only find one who will wash us clean, but one who also wants to embrace us and speak words of tenderness to us. Only then will sex take its proper order in the scheme of things, no longer as a substitute for the Father but as an echo of an intimacy we already know.

Hacking through the Jungle

Understanding all of this is a beginning; but we still have to make forward progress. We still have to find a way out of the jungle of sexual insanity. How do we do this? How do we even start? We start by simply stopping.

I remember hearing a woman tell her story of being lost in the jungle. She was first sexually abused by her father, and then after her parents divorced, she lived in a chaotic home brought on by her mother's steady stream of boyfriends. Later, in an effort to find any sense of desirability as a woman, she started to give herself to men sexually. On top of this, she covered over several pregnancies with abortions. When the jungle finally began to suffocate her, she remembers hearing the Lord say, "How can I heal you if you're not willing to heal yourself?"

That's the first step. We have to try to stop the madness, no matter how hard, even if we fail in the attempts at first. For the failure itself will teach us to draw close to the Father for both the cleansing and the strength to try again.

There is an additional step to negotiate before we can break out of the jungle. We need to come clean before others, for our sexual insanity is often laced with shame and fear of exposure before others, over what we've done. Just so, shame can only be undone in the presence of others. We cannot heal ourselves of shame. Moreover, the experience of sex, in terms of its effect on the brain, is similar to the impact of cocaine. Drug addicts need help to break free, and so do those who have been addicted to some sexual habit. And while coming clean before others may seem unthinkable, staying in the jungle of sexual insanity is what's truly unthinkable. Sadly, many church environments add to the insanity by their silence. The jungle only grows thicker.

I have had the privilege of helping to break the silence in the church I am a part of. In the men's groups I lead, each man learns to tell his heart story, including his struggles with sex. Often they share with some level of shame and fear of rejection. Yet the unexpected response from the other men is empathy and compassion. Shame is reversed as these men learn to see themselves through the eyes of love.

In one of these groups, I heard the story of a man who experienced sexual abuse at a summer camp. At the age of twelve, he was fondled by an older boy who was acting as the cabin leader. The desire to be liked by this older boy drove him to submit to an act that brought tremendous confusion and shame. He made a vow that night: "I will never let anyone else make me look stupid again." That vow drove much of his behavior for years, compelling him to avoid any relational risk. There was too much pain attached to the idea of intimacy. As he told his story to the group, the men responded with sadness and empathy. (I also felt some anger. How could that older boy inflict such a terrible act on my friend?) As we spoke all of this back to him, he began to see himself through our eyes. That boyhood event was losing its crushing shame.

Climbing the Foothill

When I was in college, I took on one of the riskiest adventures of my life. I chose to be part of a winter survival school in the Adirondack Mountains of New York. It was cold, really cold. In the seven days we spent out in the snowy wilderness, the temperature never got above twenty degrees, and one night it plunged to twenty-six *below*. Everything froze, including our peanut butter and even our toothpaste. An unprotected canteen of water turned rock solid in fifteen minutes. Every day it snowed six inches or more on top of an already deep snowpack. We had to maneuver on cross-country skis, following the portage trails that took us from one frozen lake to another. Along the way, we learned to hack out our daily water from foot-thick ice, build igloos out of packed-down snow, and avoid the ever-present danger of frostbite.

I will never forget the day we learned basic orienteering. We were given a topographical map, a compass, a few tips, and then told to find our way to the top of a designated mountain. With no trails and several feet of snow, we only had the map and compass to trust. After hours of toiling up ravines and snowdrifts on our snowshoes, we came to a summit in the early afternoon, excited that we had accomplished the task. Our team leader, who had been quiet the whole way up, then broke the news to us. We had only climbed a foothill; the real peak lay off to the left. I remember feeling so discouraged at our mistake. Yet I was invigorated for another push because for the first time I could see the peak we were supposed to climb.

After an hour or so, we approached the top, only to be forced to abandon our snowshoes. What remained of the climb was a scramble over rocks coated in ice and snow. Soon we were not only on the summit but climbing a lookout tower we found there. I will never forget the exhilaration of success, the icicles hanging from my beard, the wind whipping in my face, and the Adirondack peaks stretching out before me in all of their snowy grandeur.

I tell this story because it's such a parallel to this landmark. No matter what path we choose to take to overcome our own sexual insanity, it's not where the real peak lies. The confusion here is understandable, for the sense of shame and guilt that comes with this landmark can easily convince us that this must be the center of our sadness. But once the guilt begins to clear, once the shame begins to lift, we can see something that was obscured before. On my snowy ascent that day, I had no idea where the real peak stood until I had reached the foothill. In the same way, only when we reach the foothill of sexual sanity can we see the real summit ahead, the one we must now climb: becoming true men and women.

> Only when we reach the foothill of sexual sanity can we see the real summit ahead, the one we must now climb: becoming true men and women.

Finding Man, Finding Woman

The foundational description of mankind in the Bible is that we are male and female, created together to be a living illustration of God. A man is to reflect more of the strength and power of God while a woman is to mirror more of His beauty and tenderness. Of course a woman can exhibit strength, and should at times, and a man needs to show tenderness. But these are not at the core. Sexual intercourse then becomes a physical reenactment of this reflection. A man at erection feels strong and powerful, and a woman must become vulnerable and open to receive him. But what is true about sex is to be true in all of life. Man and woman together are to reflect the God who is both sovereign in His power and tender in His love.

It would then make sense that the fall is the shattering of this foundation. Cut off from our source of life, we do not feel like men or women at our core. Everything we do then becomes a frantic pursuit to recover that sense. With the man, it's all about attempting to feel strong, whether it's his physique, his reputation, his skill set, or his accomplishments. For a woman, beauty and love are central to her. Is she attractive? Can she find love? All of her relational manipulation and fixation on appearance appear to be ways to answer that. But for both man and woman, these are mirages,

> Man and woman together are to reflect the God who is both sovereign in His power and tender in His love.

false hopes, leading to more disappointment, more thirst, and finally despair.

Our sexual insanity is a part of this mirage. A man keeps escaping into a world of pornographic images because there he feels strong. There he can fantasize about a woman who would never reject him. A woman looking for love will give her body away to men in the hope that someone—anyone—will love her and make her feel beautiful. Yet when we de-eroticize our sexual obsessions, we find an aching heart underneath, crying out for identity. What we want so badly is to know who we really are as men and women. That's the real peak. That's the real summit. And for that we must turn elsewhere.

In the first book of C. S. Lewis's classic series, *The Chronicles of Narnia*, there is a coronation scene at the end of the story. Aslan crowns the four Pevensie children after they have helped him dethrone the White Witch. But in the actual crowning, there is an odd reversal. Each child is given a name in stark contrast to the character lapses portrayed in the story. Lucy, who was naive and childish, is called The Valiant One. Susan, who was harsh and unforgiving, is named The Gentle. Edmund, who betrayed his siblings at one point, is called The Just. And Peter, who had often been too terrified to lead, is named The Magnificent. Underneath the failures lay their true identity. Underneath the shame lay their glory. Only Aslan could see it, and only he could call it out.

Who are we then as men and women? There is only One who knows. There is only one voice that can call out the man, only one voice that can call forth the woman. It's a voice that has been calling us all our lives. But we have not known how to listen. That's where the next landmark takes us.

Part 2

MAKING THE TURN

Then as he had kept watch Sam had noticed that at times a light seemed to be shining faintly within; but now the light was even clearer and stronger. Frodo's face was peaceful, the marks of fear and care had left it; but it looked old, old and beautiful, as if the chiseling of the shaping years was now revealed in many fine lines that had before been hidden, though the identity of the face was not changed. Not that Sam Gamgee put it that way to himself. He shook his head, as if finding words useless, and murmured: "I love him. He's like that, and sometimes it shines through, somehow. But I love him, whether or no."

—J. R. R. TOLKIEN, *THE TWO TOWERS*

Landmark #5

IDENTITY

Who am I? They mock me, these lonely questions of mine.
Whoever I am, Thou knowest, O God, I am Thine!

—DIETRICH BONHOEFFER

The secret of your own heart you can never know;
but you can know Him who knows its secret.

—GEORGE MACDONALD

After all these years, I could still take you to the place on the sidewalk where it happened. I was in the eighth grade and had concluded that I needed a personality make-over. The seventh grade had not been kind to me. I was a classic geek then with all the accessories: thick glasses, straight As, and a quiet demeanor. I did my homework, practiced the piano, and collected stamps. But this sort of life was not making me a candidate for the Mr. Cool award. I needed to do something different, even drastic, so the makeover began.

First I had to find a sport to play. My attempts at basketball had been a disaster, football terrified me, and I knew nothing about baseball. So I decided to go out for the track team. I ended up being pretty fast. In fact, I became one of the fastest sprinters on the team. My status began to rise.

The next step was to hone my sarcasm so I could join the popular guys when they trashed the teachers or put down other students who lacked the cool factor. Along with that, I attempted to become funny, to always make the stupid joke, so that I could be the center of attention.

Finally, I had to figure out how to mingle with all of the various cliques. It seemed there were certain things you had to do or say to make yourself acceptable. So, I spent much of that year trying to figure out what everyone wanted and then offered that. But walking between classes one morning, I knew that despite all my efforts, my makeover was not working. I was not any happier. In fact, I was more miserable than ever. I was like a chameleon changing colors on demand. And there on that sidewalk, the disturbing question surfaced: "Who am I?"

> It seemed there were certain things you had to do or say to make yourself acceptable.

My response was just as disturbing. I had no answer.

The question resurfaced during college with greater urgency. It was the end of my sophomore year, and I was wrestling with questions of career, identity, and faith. Depression was also beginning to wrap itself around me like a dark, cold blanket. I felt lost and alone. So I decided to take a hike in the Appalachian Mountains. There, in the solitude, I hoped to find myself, to figure out who I was and what I believed. But as the hike progressed, the questions just kept swirling in my head, plunging me further down into a black hole. I was so internally focused that I barely remember anything I saw. By the end of the hike, the same disturbing feeling from the eighth grade had grown to near panic. I had no more answers at the end of that day than when I began.

The Final Descent

The question of identity doesn't just come up in our own personal stories. It also functions as the driving theme behind so many fictional ones. In *The Bourne Identity*, Jason Bourne, a highly trained CIA agent, is wounded in a failed mission, tumbles into a stormy ocean, and is hauled onto a fishing vessel, unconscious and barely alive. He wakes up terrified and disoriented, having lost his memory. To recover, he takes on the daily life of a fisherman with the rest of the crew. But it doesn't completely cure him. He can remember facts and figures, and he can remember his agent training. But in the most important matter of all, he is absolutely clueless. He doesn't know who he is. In one pathetic scene, he looks in a mirror and asks in French and German for an answer to his identity. But the response is silence.

This is a good parallel to our present situation. Often we feel as if we have been plunged into the turbulent ocean of life where we quickly become disoriented and emotionally nauseous. We have some skills to offer, and we ache to do something valuable, but the deepest part of us is lost. We have forgotten who we are. And we don't know where to look.

With this fifth landmark we begin the search. And by doing so, we descend into our deepest core, for our sense of identity is the substructure of our hearts, the very foundation of our souls. Finding an identity is thus not a casual question we can put off. Our existence pivots on what we think about ourselves. Every day, in one way or another, we live out who we think we are.

> Our existence pivots on what we think about ourselves. Every day, in one way or another, we live out who we think we are.

Oddly enough, something so crucial is also something we rarely think about. It's a bit like wearing contacts. We spend all of our waking moments looking *through* them, not *at* them. The only time we even think about looking at our lenses is when we take them out. In the same way, we see *through* the lens of our identity at life around us, but taking out the lens to examine it rarely occurs to us. It can also raise troubling questions we would rather not entertain: *What if I'm not the person I've always tried to be? What if I've been looking through the wrong lens?*

But remember that this same uneasiness was also a part of the descent of the previous landmarks. We know now we have to push through the discomfort and anxiety, so we press ahead. And our first step forward is to recognize that we cannot find ourselves *by ourselves*. Our sense of identity is never self-fabricated. It comes from the outside, from the voices we have listened to. What have those voices been telling us?

The Voices We Listen To

The first voice that shapes our identity is the voice of the shamer. It belongs to those significant people in our lives who have used their power over us in humiliating ways. We are left feeling exposed and undone by their words. We then resign ourselves to the role they cast for us or expend enormous energy vowing to escape it.

One of my faculty colleagues once told me the story of an eighth-grade girl whose life was forever altered by two words. One of the players on the middle school football team one day whispered in her ear, "You're fat." Coming from a boy of such high social standing, the shame felt annihilating. To compensate, she knew what she had to do. For the next ten years, she took the perilous path of eating disorders, a path that nearly took her life.

On another occasion, a student came to seek my counsel at the beginning of his junior year. He was from a broken home where his father had left the marriage for another woman. Due in large part to his family situation, this young man had struggled through high school both socially and academically. As he began to tell me about his summer experience, the conversation moved to a recent discussion he'd had with his father. Through tears, he repeated to me the shaming words his dad had uttered, "You are a failure at school. You will never make anything out of yourself." I tried my best to comfort him, but I don't think I was very helpful. What his father had said seemed too true to deny. After all, he really felt like a failure in so many ways. Sadly, he graduated from high school still struggling, still failing, living out the way his father had defined him.

Along with the shamer, there is another damaging voice, the affirmer. This may seem odd because we generally think of affirmation as a positive thing. And it is, *if* it's based on intimacy and connection. But affirmation based on performance easily becomes a nightmare. Our craving for validation becomes frustrated by failure or momentarily satisfied by success. Either way the trap is set. We unknowingly become tethered to a certain behavior in a frantic scheme to keep the affirmation coming. Ironically, success only makes things worse. It just keeps resetting the trap tighter each time.

I had a friend in seminary who had been a basketball star in his home state of Indiana, where the basketball gym can approach the status of a religious temple. He had been the big man on campus in both high school and college, the one everyone wanted to be like. But when he felt the call to the ministry and entered seminary, suddenly no one knew him or cared about his basketball skills. He slipped into a deep depression. All his life he had listened to his affirmers, believing that his identity was somehow linked to an orange ball. But who was he without that affirmation? He had no idea.

Another woman I know also felt chained by the voice of the affirmer. Her father was a busy surgeon disconnected from the family, so her mother held the keys to any possible affirmation. She learned from an early age that her social etiquette and outward appearance were the only ways to garner any kind of praise from her mother. But even then the anticipated praise only came in the backwards form of criticism. Once, on a high school tour of New

> Affirmation based on performance easily becomes a nightmare.

York City, she was able to attend a Broadway theater. Somehow her mother found out how she had dressed for the evening. When she returned home after the tour, she was scolded by her mother for wearing too formal a dress. On another occasion, the daughter was caught lying at school. When her mother was informed, she dismissed it with little comment. Apparently truth-telling was not a part of the etiquette needed in order to be affirmed. The daughter was always left in confusion, trying to fit a mold she never quite got. She was set up to fail.

There is a third and final voice we often listen to in our search for identity, one that is quite different from the first two. It is a voice that is simply no voice at all, the voice of silence. With no one speaking into us, we are left to ourselves to make some sense of our lives, and what we inevitably end up believing is that we are unworthy of anyone's attention. What makes this voice so damning is that it is so tricky to pinpoint. At least the shaming voice nags predictably and the affirming voice soothes, even if just for a moment. But the voice of silence is a cipher, a nothing. Often those who live with this void have some vague sense that something is

> With no one speaking into us, we are left to ourselves to make some sense of our lives, and what we inevitably end up believing is that we are unworthy of anyone's attention.

amiss, but they have no idea what it is. There is nothing definite to point to, no voice, just a silence that slowly consumes them.

Taking Off the Contacts

It's a start to understand the voices we generally listen to, but it's not enough. We need to understand what those voices have specifically said to us. And to do this, we have to attempt something that feels very different. Remember that our sense of identity functions somewhat like a contact lens. We see all of life through it. But we've never looked at it. Like a contact, we now have to take it out and examine it, perhaps for the first time. But how exactly do we do this? We do it by becoming aware of the voices in the daily stuff of life.

Something troubling happens in your normal routine, and you start reacting in the usual pattern. But instead of tumbling into the old rut, this time you stop and try to pay attention to what's underneath your reaction. What comes up may surprise you. For example, you get an unexpected expense thrown your way. Worry mutates into fear, which quickly swells into panic. You start the usual scheming and plotting. But this time you stop and ask yourself why you are reacting like this. And in that moment of quiet, this thought pops out: *I'm on my own.*

No one will ever take care of me. Really? Where did that come from?

Consider another scenario. You have a boyfriend whom you've grown to love deeply; you're starting to dream about being married to him. You are concerned that he seems to lack confidence, especially when it comes to making hard decisions, but you've been able to overlook that flaw so far. Then he does make a hard decision, one about your relationship. He ends it. You are left bewildered and hurting. In the past you've snuffed out disappointments with more exercise at the gym or more trips to the mall. But this time you choose to sit in the pain and wait. What surfaces is something you've never voiced before: *It's all my fault. Everything that happens is always my fault.* Is that really true? How did you come to believe that?

It doesn't have to be a huge crisis. Smaller events can also be revealing, like feeling rage in a traffic snarl, arguing with your spouse, or even losing your keys. Where we go with these events betrays so much of our true view about ourselves. Instead of responding in the usual ways, we need to stop, take off the contacts, and look at them. For the first time, we can now do something very different. We can listen to a new voice, the voice of truth.

Listening to the Truth

I recently taught a class about the typical struggles men experience. Before class began one evening, I was chatting with an acquaintance who had arrived early. As the starting time approached, I looked around the room and realized that there were only a handful of men present. I resumed my conversation with my friend, but inside of me a familiar feeling began to emerge, a pressure mixed with some low-level anxiety. The pressure momentarily lifted each time another man walked into the classroom. As I put words to the pressure I was feeling, this is what came up: *No one is going to show up. I will be exposed as a failure.*

This was the resurrection of my old belief structure where identity was chained to success, where public failure became public humiliation. But this time I was able to put words to it and push back with the truth: failure doesn't define me. What defines me is my connection to my Father as His true son. And then I did something I could have never imagined myself doing in years past. I simply told the class what just happened to me. I went public with my heart.

This type of maneuver was only possible because I had already taken out the contacts and looked at them. I had already understood how much I had let fear consume me and failure define me. I had seen the lie of such a storyline and the devastation it had produced in my relationships. And only after I had admitted all of this was I ready to listen to the truth. For only when the lie is exposed can the truth counter. Only when the heart is open can the truth heal.

But as we start to listen to the truth, we will become increasingly aware of a new sadness. We will see a terrible chasm—a rift between what we say we believe and what we truly believe. It is the split between the belief system we hold in our minds and the one deeply entrenched in our hearts. It is what I have termed "The Great Divide," and one of the clearest examples of it comes from the pages of the New Testament.

> For only when the lie is exposed can the truth counter. Only when the heart is open can the truth heal.

The Pharisees of Jesus' day were not the violent, hardened bunch as they are often portrayed. On the contrary, they would fit right in with most churches today. They were respectable, hard-working, well-educated men who really sought to do what was right. They knew the Old Testament backward and forward. They were role models in synagogue attendance and tithes. They were incredibly zealous to obey God. But they also hated Jesus. And they found a way to kill Him.

This should make us pause. Like the Pharisees, can we construct a religious system that shields us from the living God? It's not only possible; it happens all the time. How? By not listening to the truth.

For me, it happened this way. I spent years accumulating a storehouse of biblical and theological knowledge. I bought commentaries on every book in the Bible. I wrote pages of detailed notes on the Greek and Hebrew texts of the Bible. I read volumes of theology. I did all of this with the belief that the mere accumulation of knowledge would change my heart and the hearts of my listeners. It's not that I didn't try to apply all that knowledge. I really did. I tried earnestly. But I just couldn't listen to the truth because my heart had become bound up, calloused over, and shut down through years of shame and alienation. So I compensated by listening with all that was left, my intellect. The Great Divide grew inside of me until I fell in it and my life fell apart. I then realized that despite all my best intentions, I was clueless on how to listen to truth. I had become a Pharisee.

> I then realized that despite all my best intentions, I was clueless on how to listen to truth. I had become a Pharisee.

To go forward, I had to begin listening intently for the voices that had defined me. I had to come clean with all the messiness I had hidden for years. I had to journey through the first four landmarks with all their imbedded dangers and risks. With all that sadness and confusion out in the open, I began to read the Bible with different eyes, with my heart open and longing. *What would God say to me now? What truth would He give me?* It was a very different feeling. I began to fill my journals with Scripture that was coming alive in new ways. Old rusty cogs that had been frozen for years began to move again. I was coming alive in places I didn't even know were dead. It was a revolution.

Just recently, I was reading Jesus' memorable words: "No one knows the Son except the Father, and no one knows the Father except the Son and anyone to whom the Son desires to reveal Him. Come to Me, all of you who are weary and burdened, and I will give you rest" (Matt. 11:27–28). With my heart opened, I realized that this is what I have longed for all my life, to be pulled into a great intimacy, a great revealing, to be invited into the heart of all things, to know the Father as Jesus sees Him, and to find my rest there. I saw that I can begin to enter this rest any day, any time, by just coming to Jesus. That morning I was listening to the truth, and The Great Divide closed a bit more.

Listening to God's Voice

There is one more voice we need to listen to if we are to truly grasp our identity. It is the voice behind the Bible, the voice behind the truth, the very voice of God. The reason this is so critical is quite simple. Who else knows us better? Who understands all the quirks and wonders about us? Our parents may have a good clue, yet ultimately they cannot see everything about us. Only God can. When Heidi and I speak to our daughters about the time before they were born, we often tell them that they were in God's thoughts. But this leads to some arresting questions. What was God thinking when He thought of you? What was He looking for? What did He desire? What was He trying to express? These are no dreamy speculations for those with nothing better to do. These questions penetrate to the very heart of our identity confusion.

> What was God thinking when He thought of you? What was He looking for? What did He desire? What was He trying to express?

We certainly need to know that we are sons and daughters of the living God through Jesus Christ. Walking in that truth is a necessary beginning that challenges our usual sense of abandonment or aloneness. But it's still generic. What we really ache to know is who we are individually before Him, that He knows us by name. For identity comes only through connection. And maybe, just maybe, God has been trying to connect to us. Maybe He has been trying to speak to us about our true identity. And maybe we just haven't known how to listen.

There is ample evidence in Scripture to support such a contention. Jesus often appended this simple statement to His teachings: "Anyone who has ears should listen!" (Matt. 11:15, for example). Taken literally, this sounds ridiculous. Who doesn't have physical ears? But of course, this is not what Jesus is implying. What He is referring to is how easy it is to miss what He is saying. To really hear Jesus requires concentration. To really understand Him requires attention. Perhaps we cannot only miss His truth in Scripture; we can also miss His voice in our hearts.

But if we are attentive, if we quiet ourselves to listen, the truth can come to us, and not just generically. It can come to us in a voice, in a person, speaking into our hearts with an intimate knowledge of our joys and sorrows. It doesn't change the truth of what He has spoken in the Scriptures. But the voice here speaks as someone who truly understands our hearts.

Sometimes when wandering through a mall, Heidi and I will run across one of those back-massage machines that are set out for public use. She can select the type of massage she wants and then let the machine do its work. But as good as those machines may be, they lack the personal touch. What she really enjoys are the back massages I give her. I know her aches and pains, the muscles that kink, the spots that tighten, and how much pressure to apply. I know these things just because I know her after all these years of marriage. How God comes to us is very much like this. The truth of the Scripture is certainly compelling when we learn to listen to it with our hearts open and longing. But to have the Father personally massage our hearts, knowing intimately our aches and pains, is a consolation with no parallel. He wants us to know that He feels our sadness and confusion. He wants us to be free in the truth. He wants us to know who we are.

We just need to listen.

I once went through a season of wrestling with shame. I had taken off the contacts and identified how shame had directed my life and had run me down. I also knew that Jesus had borne not only my sin on the cross, but my shame as well. But the shame was so pervasive that I couldn't shake it off. Even after trying to listen to the truth here for a long time, I was still held in its grip. I was struggling to listen to God, but nothing seemed to come. Then one night, as I lay somewhere between consciousness and sleep, these words suddenly struck like a lightning bolt: "Shame has kept you from love, and only love will heal you of shame." Those fourteen words were both a summary of my life and a light pointing out the path I needed to follow. They were something only the Father could know, something only He could personally say to me. But I needed more.

A month or so later it came as I sat in a coffee shop in Chicago, journaling and wrestling once again with shame. This time I heard Jesus say to me quietly, "Bill, just give Me your shame." It seems so obvious to me now, but I had never really let Him take the burden of my shame. Tearfully, I listed all the shameful events of my life, and one by one I simply put them on Jesus. It was a remarkable moment. Shame began to lose its grip. Instead, what Jesus says about me became what mattered. And He is not ashamed of me, or ashamed to call me His brother (Heb. 2:11). That's who I really am.

> Shame has kept you from love, and only love will heal you of shame.

The listening continues. My journals have become the record of struggling to hear God's voice. Sometimes He will speak general reminders to me of His presence: *I am here. I am with you.* Other times the encouragement will be more specific: *You are Mine. You are My brave son.* And other times He gently prods me: *I must have it all. Follow Me today.* Finally at surprising moments He will probe me with a question. Once I was struggling with a men's group I was leading, concerned about whether the group was going to succeed. As I wrestled with my fears into the night, this is what came to me: *Are you willing to fight for them?* It was a sharp reminder to get the focus off of myself.

This is the type of thing that can happen as we begin to listen to God's voice. Our identity gets grounded in our connection to Him. It's so extraordinary that it will be pursued further in the seventh landmark. But first, we must turn our attention elsewhere.

Jason Bourne spent all three movies of the Bourne trilogy fighting to unearth his true identity. Just so, finding our true identity and living out of it will not come without a battle. For there is another voice we have been listening to all our lives, often without realizing it. It's dark, foreboding, and sinister. And it's the next landmark.

Part 3

ASCENDING INTO LIFE

He longed to forgive everyone and for everything, and to beg
forgiveness. Oh, not for himself, but for all men, for all and for
everything. "And others are praying for me too," echoed again
in his soul. But with every instant he felt clearly and, as it were,
tangibly, that something firm and unshakable as that vault of
heaven had entered into his soul. It was as though some idea
had seized the sovereignty of his mind—and it was for all his
life and forever and ever. He had fallen on the earth a weak boy,
but he rose up a resolute champion.

—FYODOR DOSTOEVSKY, *THE BROTHERS KARAMAZOV*

Landmark #6

BATTLE

Gradually it was disclosed to me that the line separating good and evil passes not through states, nor between classes, nor between political parties either—but right through every human heart—and through all human hearts.

—ALEKSANDR I. SOLZHENITSYN

And though this world with devils filled, Should threaten to undo us, We will not fear, for God hath willed His truth to triumph through us.

—MARTIN LUTHER

I will never forget the first time I watched the movie *Saving Private Ryan*. I had heard many others speak to me about it before I finally decided to see it for myself. After I put in the DVD and turned off the lights, I soon entered a world of unimaginable devastation. The D-Day landing on Omaha Beach is portrayed in such horrific detail that I almost felt I was there. The mangled bodies, the cries of the wounded, the unrelenting gunfire, the exploding land mines, the sickening chaos—I was drawn in and repulsed by what I saw on the screen. It was the reality of war.

I have had this experience many times viewing other war movies, such as *Band of Brothers, Platoon,* and *Glory.* As I have watched, I have found myself asking the same questions over and over. *What would I have done? How would I have dealt with the fear? How would I have handled the trauma?* We see the main characters not only wrestle with physical challenges and moral dilemmas, we watch them emotionally harden just to survive the onslaught of war. It's riveting, and it's heartbreaking.

But once the movie ends, I turn the lights back on and reenter my normal world of work, errands, bike riding, and cleaning the gutters. The questions those war movies provoke are interesting to ponder, but I don't live in that world. Or so I think.

One night Heidi came home from a gathering of women nearly too overwhelmed to describe some of their life scenarios. There were women whose husbands had left the home and abandoned the family. Others had gone through horrific divorces, and still others had troubled marriages, exhausting them after years of strain.

This made me think of a certain group of men I had recently come to know. We gathered weekly to share our joys and struggles and what God is teaching us. Some of their backgrounds include addiction to pornography, addiction to alcohol, fathers who abused them physically and emotionally, and fathers who just left. Yet the men in this group are no monsters. They are good men with respectable careers and ministries. I have come to appreciate all of them and their courage in telling their stories.

Add to this many other stories I know of, stories of college friends and seminary buddies, stories of students and parents, stories of abandonment and abuse, stories of mangled hearts and devastated lives. And then I look in the mirror at my own life and see the scars I bear.

> And it hits me. I'm not watching a war movie anymore. I'm in one.

And it hits me. I'm not watching a war movie anymore. I'm in one.

Waking Up

I admit this can seem so overly dramatic. Even I have difficulty believing it sometimes. Over a recent holiday break, I enjoyed several days of rest and peace, filled with simple joys and warm conversations. The highlight came on Christmas morning when our family opened gifts by a crackling fire. We took our time sipping coffee, nibbling on coffee cake, and watching the snow jostled by the winter wind. While all this was going on, I remembered that I had been teaching a class on the topic of spiritual battle a few days earlier. Yet on that morning the idea of war seemed a million miles away. I wondered whether I had exaggerated my point. Maybe life isn't so combative after all.

I now know that I was being lulled to sleep by a spell I have often felt, one that is hard to resist. For awakening to the battle is a part of the battle itself. For there are multiple forces at work, trying first to put us asleep and then ensuring matters so that we stay that way.

> For awakening to the battle is a part of the battle itself.

Our fallen self is one of those culprits. We are easily led astray by the seductive pull to make this life an Eden again. I once saw an advertisement for a new beach community in Florida. The ad featured pictures of golfers touring manicured fairways, lovers walking on spotless beaches, and families eating gourmet dinners. And of course, everyone was smiling. It looked like heaven. But what really caught my attention was the tagline: "Life made effortless." There it was again, the pull back to Eden. We want life to be easy, peaceful, and effortless.

And we think that if we work hard enough and make enough money, it will finally come to us. But we are deceived.

The world is another force, constantly promoting this deception by appealing to our lost happiness. If we buy this shampoo or follow this advice or purchase this car or eat this food, life will finally come together for us. We will find the peace that we long for. (If you take a moment and channel surf, you will be startled at the tidal wave of images and words that preach the same message.) We are constantly being offered solutions to our longings, usually with a price tag. The one thing we are never told is that to find peace we must enter a war.

A final force at work keeping us asleep is the devil himself, whose cruel tactics are both subversive and cunning. He deftly bends reality so that comments about spiritual battle seem foolish or antiquated. Then he twists things so that appeals to our happiness and ease feel warranted, persuasive, even irresistible. We are often unaware that we are under attack because he likes to work covertly, so as to keep the upper hand. And a part of that strategy is to make sure that we stay asleep to his operations.

> The one thing we are never told is that to find peace we must enter a war.

The apostle Paul urges us to wake up from our slumber because our salvation is nearer than when we first believed. We are to "discard the deeds of darkness" (Rom. 13:12). Reading on in the same sentence, we may expect the text to say something like "and take up the deeds of righteousness," but that's not where it goes. Instead, we are to "discard the deeds of darkness" so that we can "put on the armor of light." It seems that our idols and vices have affected us like sleeping pills, drugging us so that we can't see the war raging around us. So when the shooting starts, we're taken out before we even know what's going on. But if we're awake, we'll have enough sense to put on the armor. At least then we'll have a fighting chance.

Now we begin to see what this landmark is all about. It's a part of the ascent, a call to wake up to the battle around us. But it will be a risk. It will require things of us we're not sure we're ready for. It may call us to a new level of discipline or self-sacrifice. We may be tempted to hit the snooze button and pretend that none of this is happening.

But isn't sleeping in a war a greater risk?

A Short Briefing

If we do decide to wake up, we'll need some basic knowledge on military strategy. Warfare is often engineered around an understanding of how the enemy operates. If we understand the tactics of the opposing side, perhaps we won't be so easily ambushed. And perhaps we can find weak places to exploit. So we need a briefing on the enemy.

Paul refers to the schemes of the devil as something we need to stand against (Eph. 6:13). What exactly are those schemes?

His first one is accusation. In fact, the name Satan means "one who accuses." Here he intensifies the condemnation or shame we may feel and then mixes in our own fallen story lines to produce a sickening concoction we feel compelled to drink. We are literally poisoned by his vicious words: "You are unworthy of anyone's love. You don't deserve anything better. You're scum and your heart is worthless. You are such a weak man. You are such an ugly woman. It's all your fault. No one would ever be interested in your heart." On and on it goes. And the accusations aren't just meant to make us uncomfortable. Their purpose is to maim, cripple, and then destroy. Also notice that the devil aims straight for our identity. If he can make us swallow these accusations, we are easy prey for whatever else he may hurl at us.

The next scheme the devil uses is deception. His tactic here is to make the truth look like a lie. What God offers us is presented as boring, lifeless, or simply untrustworthy. Then he turns the tables so that what he offers looks fun, lifegiving, or too obvious to be denied. With great precision, he appeals to those exact places in our hearts that have been already weakened by his accusations. We seem ripe to receive what will only lead to more death and destruction in our lives.

A final scheme involves temptation. Once he has planted the deception, then it becomes a boxing match. A good boxer knows how to exploit a cut by pummeling it relentlessly until it becomes a gash and then a bleeding wound. That's how the enemy uses temptation on us. The accusations and deceptions exhaust us. We are left tottering, trying to keep our balance. Then we get battered with temptation until we can no longer stand. We give in. And what happens next? The accusation starts over again, the deception, the temptation. But this time the schemes cut deeper. More mutilation is done. It's ruthless and sadistic. There is no mercy, no timeout. It's war.

> It's ruthless and sadistic. There is no mercy, no timeout. It's war.

One further detail in this briefing: his schemes come to us in two general ways. One of them is a whisper of thoughts that are injected into our stream of thinking. Perhaps you have assumed that everything that runs through your mind is your own. Perhaps you need to think again. Remember, staying covert is a part of the devil's tactics. The second is what I call nonverbal shoving. These are the pulls we feel at times that try to drag us like a riptide out into the ocean, the one place we don't want to go. To resist seems futile. Letting ourselves be dragged along feels like the only option at the time. And the shoving can be so difficult to pinpoint and resist precisely because it is nonverbal. There are no words to it, and seemingly no words to counter it.

Assault Story Number One

Here's a personal story from the battlefield. I spoke one Sunday on this very topic, and whenever I teach about the battle, I am keenly aware of the possibility of assault. But even my heightened sense of alert did not prepare me for what was about to be unleashed.

The battle commenced during the church service immediately after my talk. As I watched the various worship leaders and speakers, critical thoughts about them were at first suggested to me and then flung at me in rapid-fire succession. "The music is too showy. Everyone is up there just to get the applause. The speaker has nothing worthwhile to say." Sadly, a few of my good friends were a part of those leading up front. No sooner would I fend off one thought than another would be fired. I left church wearied and disoriented.

When I arrived home, Heidi found me in the back bedroom and closed the door to speak to me in private. I could see the hurt in her eyes. She told me that she felt sorry for me, sorry that I felt so isolated that I rarely mentioned her or our children in my teaching. It seemed to be all about me. The old lie that I had to figure out life on my own had come back to haunt me again, this time damaging my closest relationships. She spoke the truth I needed to hear, but my disorientation from church had already left me vulnerable. Now it quickly shifted to shame. I felt raw and exposed. And when shame comes to me, it tunnels inward and morphs into self-condemnation. This time the enemy took my usual pattern and just turned up the volume. The accusations that came to me were deafening. *What right do I have to stand in front of anyone and teach anything when I am such a mess? I am such a failure.* I wanted to crawl into bed and hide. But I couldn't because there were college students from church coming over to our house for lunch. In fact, they were already there. *How was I going to interact with them? How could I fake it?* I realized then that I was in a brutal battle. Only two hours after speaking about this very topic, I was coming unglued. I stood in the bedroom and prayed feverishly, trying to regain my composure. I then walked into the kitchen to meet our guests, still shaken but determined to go on.

As I mingled with students, the darkness lifted a little. I had survived. The battle was over. Or so I thought.

Later that afternoon I went to a recreation center to swim laps for a little exercise and relaxation. After I had come home, I realized that my wallet was not where I usually keep it in my desk. I went out to the car to search, still feeling weak from the earlier battles and asking God to help me find it. But the wallet wasn't there. I walked back into the house, feeling the sentence of doom on me. In this final assault, the enemy once again hammered me, using shame. There are few things that make me feel as foolish as when I lose my wallet. I think that I should be responsible enough as a man to keep up with it, and when I lose it, I feel shame over my inadequacy.

This time instead of going inward, however, the shame went outward, in the form of rage. I could feel the anger rising in me like a pool of lava wanting to erupt. I was furious. I wanted to throw things. I couldn't even pray. I was going to find that wallet. I would not be defeated.

I searched through the house, quietly fuming. Nothing. I searched the normal places and then the ridiculous places. Nothing. I went out to the car I had driven to the pool and threw everything out of it onto the driveway, cursing the whole time. Still nothing. And then I stopped and dissolved into tears. *How did I get here?* Only twelve hours ago I had spoken about the battle. Now I was a complete failure, a vanquished foe.

I quit looking for the wallet, admitted my foolish anger, and told the Father that I trusted Him with it.

That prayer was the slender cord that drew me up out of the raging waters. The next morning Heidi found the wallet while making the bed. It had slipped between the bed frame and a nearby bench so that it was easily overlooked. I remember feeling relieved about recovering the wallet and then slightly hopeful. Even when the battle had been vicious, I had survived and found a way through the carnage.

Not every day is like this, of course. Some days the bombs are heard only in the distance, but at other times they drop directly overhead. Often the assaults target those places where we have been wounded in the past or use the guilt we feel over some of our most controlling idols. However the battle may start, the disorientation and accusation that come can shred any sense of our identity as the Father's beloved sons and daughters.

Fighting Back

Understanding the schemes is helpful, but we still have no idea how to fight back. That's what we need, and the apostle Paul gives us just such a battle plan in Ephesians 6:10–13. In this passage, we are told how to maintain our identity in Christ, a position that puts us far above all demonic powers and authorities. For we are bonded to Jesus in His death, burial, and resurrection, where He disarmed the evil one of his powers. It is in this place that we are asked to be strong in God's power and to prepare ourselves for battle. We may now imagine the strategy is to charge the evil one in a head-on assault or at least ambush him, but neither of these strategies are commanded. Instead we are asked to do something rather odd. We are asked to stand. "Put on the full armor of God so that you can stand against the tactics of the Devil" (Eph. 6:11).

> For we are bonded to Jesus in His death, burial, and resurrection, where He disarmed the evil one of his powers. It is in this place that we are asked to be strong in God's power and to prepare ourselves for battle.

But why stand? Why not fight on the offensive?

If this fight were merely with flesh and blood, then classic battle strategies would make sense, but we are not fighting that kind of war. The real battle does not lie in the tensions of the workplace, the nagging family conflicts, the disappointments of marriage, or the misunderstandings that can derail entire churches. Though we are easily lured into this type of thinking, this is not where the real war zone lies. Behind all of these skirmishes lies an immense, towering edifice of evil: "For our battle is not against flesh and blood, but against the rulers, against the authorities, against the world powers of this darkness, against the spiritual forces of evil in the heavens" (Eph. 6:12). We are being hunted by forces that can outmaneuver mere human intelligence and power, and we will go down unless we learn to stand.

Yet even if we accept this strategy, it still makes little sense. How do we overcome by keeping an upright posture? Well, it all depends on what you mean. It is one thing to stand up after you have been sitting down. But this is no mere standing. This is a stance of fierce resistance.

Imagine yourself caught in rapids and clinging to an overhanging branch so as not to be swept away. The attempt to stand and pull yourself up out of the raging river requires tremendous focus and a refusal to let the water take you down. This is a more accurate image of the type of standing we are asked to do. It is a fierce denial in the face of the evil one's attacks, a passionate refusal to give way. And if we stand and refuse to back down, he will finally yield. In fact, Scripture says that he must *flee* (James 4:7). Recapturing the lost places in our hearts requires this type of defiant standing. No wonder Paul repeated the instruction to stand four separate times in the same passage.

Assault Story Number Two

In the art of war, distraction is a well-known military strategy. By presenting a ruse to the enemy, we hope that he will overcommit on one front, leaving himself vulnerable for attack on another. I believe the evil one often uses such a tactic. We will be attacked in some way that causes distress, like a gnawing temptation or a repeated accusation. As the assault presses in relentlessly, we have to commit enormous emotional and mental energy just to keep from falling apart. We are left with little capacity to deal with any other battle beyond this one.

But this is a ruse. Underneath this surface conflict is the real battle where the enemy meets little or no resistance. He can inflict severe damage without even being noticed. I am not speaking in the hypothetical here; I have had a twenty-five-year battle structured along these very lines. And the reason it went on so long is that I was blind to this strategy. Here's what happened.

> Underneath this surface conflict is the real battle where the enemy meets little or no resistance. He can inflict severe damage without even being noticed.

I have always been a questioner, one whose desire for knowledge seemed endless at times. I remember wondering in early adolescence why there were so many church denominations. *If Christianity was indeed the truth, why couldn't everyone agree?* As I got older, the questions became more complex. *Did I get my beliefs about life simply because I was raised in America? How can I have any confidence in the Bible when it is dismissed by so many intellectuals? Are Buddhism or Hinduism better ways to live? Can I even know if God is real?* During college and into seminary, the battle took on an intensity that is even now difficult to express.

The questions would come at me rapid-fire, causing tremendous confusion and anxiety. I was in such distress sometimes that I became physically nauseated. Whenever I would find a reasonable answer to one question, another one would immediately appear, framed as a denial or as a contrasting spin on the issue. Sometimes I would find a really solid answer, and when the question would resurface a few months later, I seemed to forget the answer and find myself back at square one.

On top of this, I was ashamed of the questions. Being a seminary graduate and now a minister, how could I admit that the foundations of my faith appeared to be constantly tottering? Teaching apologetics, a defense of the Christian faith, only intensified the shame. I was giving out the answers, even though inwardly I was still unsure at times. The turmoil was affecting my marriage as well. When I became consumed by the questions, I disconnected from Heidi, unable to emerge from an inner world of turmoil. I felt lost. She just felt alone.

The lightbulb finally came on at a prayer retreat Heidi and I attended where a wise and seasoned spiritual counselor quietly listened to my whole story, one that I had been ashamed to tell. I explained that I had been fighting—and losing—the battle by always trying to find more answers to the questions. He bypassed all of that and went straight to the demonic. My problem was not that I didn't know enough to believe the faith with confidence. My problem was that I didn't see the cunning scheme devised against me. The point was not to keep me in doubt. That was just a ruse. The point was to keep me distracted so that I couldn't attend to the deeper issues in my heart, the coldness and disconnection, the drivenness and fear. It had worked so well for so long. But not anymore.

> My problem was not that I didn't know enough to believe the faith with confidence. My problem was that I didn't see the cunning scheme devised against me.

I began to write the questions down, and I noticed that there was a pattern to them that bordered on the obnoxious. It was almost like a child who repeats back every sentence you say just to irritate you. I realized that I would never ask them in this manner. These could not just be the questions I was asking. Instead, it was a demonic spirit that I had always assumed was my own thinking. I began to stand against it, not by trying to find more answers, but by standing in Christ. I did this repeatedly over weeks and even months, and I began to notice the questions lessen both in intensity and quantity. I also began to see that the answers I already knew were substantial, answers that satisfied both my mind and heart. And I saw that the nature of human knowledge is such that it is always limited. It is okay to believe deeply and still have questions. With that distraction set to rest, I was able for the first time to focus on other issues in my heart that desperately needed attending. I had made so little progress there because I had been so sidetracked.

> Instead, it was a demonic spirit that I had always assumed was my own thinking. I began to stand against it, not by trying to find more answers, but by standing in Christ.

But the clarity that now came was stunning. I could see. The ascent into life had begun.

And that is where we leave this landmark. We are indeed in a battle, assaulted by an enemy bent on our destruction. But we can fight back. And whatever the difficulties, whatever the pushback, the effort to stand and not give way is so worth it. This is where standing in Christ takes us. But the standing must be in the company of others. That's where we go next.

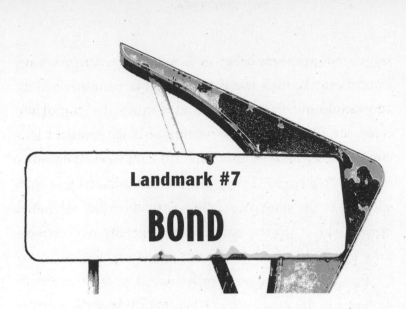

Landmark #7

BOND

You have sent forth fragrance, and I have
drawn in my breath, and I pant after You.
I have tasted You, and I hunger and thirst after You.
You have touched me, and I have burned for Your peace.

—Augustine

Be Thou my Wisdom and Thou my true Word;
I ever with Thee, and Thou with me, Lord;
Thou my great Father, I Thy true son;
Thou in me dwelling, and I with Thee one.

—Ancient Irish Hymn

It was my fourteenth year of coaching cross-country. It began like all the other years, a sleepy group of high school runners gathered for an early morning practice in June. The team would then spend the rest of that summer logging countless miles before heading off to camp where I put them through five days of intense running, biking, and swimming that climaxed in a mini-triathlon. After camp we shifted into our routine of daily practices and weekly meets. All of this rolled on for several months until the big regional race that determined if we would advance to the state meet. This particular year, we didn't quite make it, so the season was officially over. It was time for me to schedule the last practice.

But the last practice really wasn't a practice at all. Except for the new runners, everybody knew what was about to happen. The team crammed into a tiny stone bell tower that stood on one of our race sites. I said a few opening words and then invited anyone to share a memory from the season. For the next hour or so, the tower rocked with laughter. Most of the stories I already knew, but there were others the team had hidden from me until then. I laughed at those the most. But at some point the conversation took a turn into deeper waters. The seniors each began to share what the season had meant to them. What they said wasn't about meets or times or scores. Instead, they spoke about the time spent, the suffering endured, the lessons gained, and the brotherhood born. Finally, they each took a turn ringing the huge bell in the tower.

Then something happened that is forever marked in my memory. As the seniors were ringing the bell, a thunderstorm clipped the area, leaving the sun to peak out from under the towering clouds just as it was setting. It cast an intense yellowish hue everywhere, tinting the landscape with an electric glow that created a fairyland appearance. The greens of the mown fields and the reds of the fall leaves turned deeper, and then deeper still. I have never seen anything like it before or since. And then to top it off, a massive rainbow suddenly appeared. The seniors all scrambled onto the roof of the bell tower, and I hastily took group photos, framing the rainbow as if it had landed on top of their heads. Then it quickly faded and disappeared altogether. The season was over.

The seniors lingered awkwardly for several minutes, first embracing each other and then me. One of them, who had run all four years of high school, reached for me with tears freely flowing. In a choking voice, he kept repeating, "Coach, it's over. I can't believe it's over." I was surprised and drawn by his intense emotion. Here was a runner whose normal demeanor was outgoing and playful, to the point of mischievous, yet something had pierced him and left him trembling.

What this young man had tapped into was an immense gulf of desire, one that is everywhere around us and in us. Lovers are haunted by it. Families are built with it. Soldiers depend on it. Friendships endure because of it. All of us ache for it. It is what we spend our whole lives hoping for, searching for. It's the bond.

We all sense from our earliest moments that connection is life. To be abandoned and left alone is death. So

> We all sense from our earliest moments that connection is life. To be abandoned and left alone is death.

we find someone, something, anything to attach ourselves to. Here we uncover the setting for this landmark, but herein also lies the problem. It's not the reality or power of the bond. It's how we've chosen to attach ourselves.

The Original Bond

At the center of all reality is not a force or an idea. At the heart of all things is a bond. Jesus Himself described the bond as one between Himself and the Father: "The Father and I are one" (John 10:30). "The one who has seen Me has seen the Father" (John 14:9). They live in a tightly-knit connection of mutual love and delight, a love that is personified in the Holy Spirit. The Son never says or does anything that the Father doesn't first say or do. The Father, in turn, honors the Son and loves to give Him authority to judge and rule. The Son basks in the intense delight His Father has for Him, and the Father relishes the love of His Son. There is a searing intimacy here of which we only catch the radiating warmth in our own friendships and romances.

Theologically, we call it the Trinity, but essentially, it's a bond. And out of that original bond the whole story of creation was authored. We were meant in some way to be a part of that bond, but that is not our present reality. What we usually experience is disconnection. What we feel inside is a yawning abyss.

When we first met our beloved family dog in the neighborhood pound, she was one of the most pitiful sights we had ever seen. All the other dogs were yelping and jumping up for our attention, but she cowered along the back fence, trembling uncontrollably. She was so fearful that she would hardly come to us. We were told that she had probably been beaten and was found wandering the streets, hungry and alone. That's a fitting image of the disconnected human heart. Left alone, we cower and tremble. We must find connection somewhere, or we'll die.

And we do find some kind of connection, but not with the Father and Son. Precisely here is the magnetic lure of idols. They call out to us with an attraction that feels irresistible, for our idols touch the unbonded places of our hearts, the places where we feel most alone and afraid. They seduce us with the

> For our idols touch the unbonded places of our hearts, the places where we feel most alone and afraid.

momentary pleasure of attachment, wrapping their arms of comfort around us. But as time goes on, those arms squeeze tighter, bruising us and then crushing us. The bond that we thought was going to give us life begins to kill us.

But at other times, we hear a faint echo of that original bond. Perhaps it comes through a team experience, as it did with my cross-country runner. Or perhaps it happens in a moment of silence with a close friend when words are not needed. Maybe it occurs with a spouse in bed one night when the conversation moves from surface talk to the secrets of each other's hearts. Or maybe it takes place with a brother or sister while viewing forgotten pictures of a family vacation. Whatever awakens in that moment seems dangerous, unmanageable. We long for this beyond words.

> But what if we could feel that original bond again? Better yet, what if we were invited back into it?

We then spend our entire lives trying to re-create the echo that we have heard. We pursue it relentlessly and unconsciously through our careers, marriages, friendships, even in our hobbies. But what we ache for we cannot seem to grasp. It's like trying to hold water in a sieve. But what if we could feel that original bond again? Better yet, what if we were invited back into it?

The Invitation Back

Such an invitation has been issued by Jesus Himself (see John 17). Right before He descends into the horror of the cross, Jesus prays for Himself, for His disciples, and then for all who would come to believe in Him. The fact that He would think of us believers down through history is certainly comforting. But what is really startling is how He prays for us. He doesn't pray for health or strength or perseverance or safety or any of the usual things we often pray for. He prays for oneness. He prays for the bond: "I pray also for those who will believe in me . . . that all of them may be one, Father, just as you are in me and I am in you. May they also be in us so that the world may believe that you have sent me" (John 17:20–21 NIV).

The effect of Jesus' sacrifice is not just release from our idols and bondage. That would be celebration enough. But something more is given, something almost unthinkable. We are summoned back into that original bond. We are invited back home. Every

> The effect of Jesus' sacrifice is not just release from our idols and bondage. That would be celebration enough. But something more is given, something almost unthinkable. We are summoned back into that original bond. We are invited back home.

discussion I have ever heard about the Trinity is about trying to understand it. Jesus never does this. He just invites us into it.

Imagine the most beloved family you know inviting you to spend a week with them on vacation. Imagine the atmosphere, the conversation, the carefree fun. Or imagine being invited to spend a day with someone you have looked up to all your life. Maybe it's with a well-known author or speaker or just someone you have admired from afar. When I daydream about such invitations, I imagine myself asking: "Why invite me?" And then I hear this reply coming back: "Why? Because your company is desired."

Jesus' prayer for oneness is just such a dream come true. It's an invitation back into the bond between the Father and the Son because our company is desired. But the prayer doesn't stop there. We are invited back with other believers so that we can begin to enjoy together the bond that the Father and Son enjoy. It's a type of connection so rare and attractive that the world is invited to come and watch so that they can see for themselves the truth of Jesus. I have come to believe that if this type of bond were demonstrated even in small and stumbling ways, the doors of the church would be ripped open as seekers race in for a look.

But I do not see many church doors being ripped open, and I do not see many seekers racing in for a look. We are so used to being disconnected, so used to counterfeits, that this type of bond seems like a vague dream bordering on the edge of reality. Some may even feel it's just the wistful musings of an ancient mystic. But this much I know: Jesus was no dreamy mystic, and His prayers were not vague rhetoric. If He prayed for oneness, it is possible. But how?

> I have come to believe that if this type of bond were demonstrated even in small and stumbling ways, the doors of the church would be ripped open as seekers race in for a look.

Vertical Bonding

Responding to the invitation starts vertically, connecting back to God. It's the initial bond from which everything else comes. The New Testament gives some intriguing accounts of those who accepted the invitation. Here is one of them:

> More than that, I also consider everything to be a loss in view of the surpassing value of knowing Christ Jesus my Lord. Because of Him I have suffered the loss of all things and consider them filth, so that I may gain Christ and be found in Him, not having a righteousness of my own from the law, but one that is through faith in Christ. (Phil. 3:8–9)

The apostle Paul here is describing his own experience of the bond, and his code language for it is found in the phrase "in Christ." He uses that phrase over and over in his writings, circling back to it like a refrain in a long ballad. It means everything to him. It is the key to his life and what he hopes his readers will enter. For to be *in* something is more than proximity or closeness; it means to be engulfed in something, much like swimming in a vast ocean. Compared to being engulfed in the bond, everything else for Paul is filth. In fact, the word *filth* here is actually the word for human excrement. Paul is trying to shock his readers awake with the beauty of the vertical bond. Compared to it, everything else is reduced to a dung pile.

Somehow as believers, we are all supposed to enter this bond. But how?

For me, the entrance happened without my even realizing it at the time. So much of my life had been given over to seeking affirmation from others that it never occurred to me to ask the Father for it. But as I worked through the landmarks, especially the identity one, I found that *He* began to approach *me*. I had already begun to lay my heart open, allowing the words of Scripture to speak to me and soothe me. And then I began to hear His voice, a voice that I had not been able to listen to until then. What He often said were simple words of affirmation: that He loved me, that He was with me, that I belonged to

Him—all truths I had heard many times. But they weren't delivered like a lecture. They were spoken by someone who knew my story, who knew what I longed for.

And there was another way He drew toward me.

One morning I was reading the passage where Jesus calls us to take up His yoke and learn from Him (Matt. 11:28–29). He is using the familiar practice at the time of yoking an inexperienced ox with a veteran one to learn how to plow the fields. I vividly remember an image of Jesus coming to me, putting His arm around my shoulder, and sensing that this was the yoke He was offering. It would be the connection He would initiate with me if I let Him, where He could intimately guide me and train me.

Sometime later it struck me that God had approached me personally, knowing my own idiomatic language of love, for I feel loved most deeply when I hear affirming words or feel physical touch. He was personally calling me up into the bond. The invitation had my name written on it. I was beginning to *know* what the Father felt toward me, that He delights in me as a son and longs for my company.

The invitation had my name written on it. I was beginning to *know* what the Father felt toward me, that He delights in me as a son and longs for my company.

Still, to wade out into the ocean and fully answer the invitation I needed to *feel* what the Father felt toward me. I needed to experience that delight myself. I needed to sense His joy over me. So I started by simply trying to feel that delight and joy in the silence of each early morning. For someone whose whole life has been framed by disconnection, it seemed like an impossible task. This landmark loomed so far in the distance. But I persisted, and over time the disconnection began to dissolve and the bond deepened and tightened.

Horizontal Bonding

But the bond was never meant to be enjoyed alone, for Jesus didn't just pray that we as individuals would know the bond. He prayed that we would know it *together*— "that all of them may be one" (John 17:21 NIV). The vertical draw upward must also push us out horizontally. But again we face the same question as before: how do we enter this bond? I think it only happens when we decide to break our compulsive allegiance to hiding.

It's a rather obvious point, but one easily missed. You can't bond to a mask. You can't have intimacy with a front. From an early age we have all learned to one degree or another how to hide from others. I am afraid that much of what we call our personality may be more of a constructed facade built over time to make ourselves acceptable to others. Whatever makes us appear more beautiful, more appealing, more successful is what we offer to those around us. Whatever makes us look weak or ugly, we bury underground, hoping no one will ever find it.

I remember reading an essay that one of my students had written for a test. Outwardly, she was Miss Everything as a high school girl—a popular leader, a star athlete, an academic machine, and a hit with the boys. I assumed she was happy and content until I ran across something in that essay that jumped out at me. She began to describe how much she hated her life and how she pasted on a mask each day, feeling the pressure to be happy for everyone else. She wanted out desperately, but didn't know how.

Her story is in some way the struggle of every student I have ever taught. And if we continue on with the masking as adults, the fronts only get more ingrained and complicated. We put masks on top of masks. We wear them for so long that we don't even know how many there are or how to take them off. And the prospect of doing so makes us uneasy. I once asked a group of men what comes up when they think of taking off their masks. One man simply replied, "Terror."

Sadly, when we enter the life of many churches, it's not a chance to unmask. Instead we just add on another layer. This is what I call The Religious Front. On top of offering others what we hope will gain acceptance, we

> Sadly, when we enter the life of many churches, it's not a chance to unmask. Instead we just add on another layer. This is what I call The Religious Front.

now have to appear moral and holy. It's never said out loud, but it's the unspoken assumption that blows through the Sunday conversations and programs. The thought of coming out of hiding is never entertained. So the masquerade continues. So does the exhaustion.

But there is one thing for certain. The Father and Son have no religious front between them. They share a life together where there is no masquerading, no facades, no hiding—only the bond. There is no jealousy, no bitterness, no anger, no disappointment, and certainly no betrayal. They experience none of the fallout that we are so familiar with in our relationships. Why? Because there is no shame.

The Destroyer of the Bond

I once saw a movie recounting the true story of a boy who wet his bed, even into his early teen years. Despite the mother's constant nagging and the father's gentle encouragement, neither could get him to stop. So one day the mother decided to hang his yellowed bed sheets out the window each morning, thinking that the shame of being a public spectacle would eventually cure him. The first time she did this, the father was driving him home along with some of his buddies. As they pulled into the driveway, there on full display were the sheets. He was humiliated, devastated beyond words. The next day, while sitting with his buddies at lunch, he made up a story that the new family dog wasn't housebroken yet. The masking had begun. Then he quit the football team so he could sprint home after school and pull down the sheets. He was determined to do whatever it took to protect himself from further shame.

This story is such a graphic picture of the human condition. For shame is primal, the first fallen emotion recorded in Scripture. As such, it is the foundation of so many of our other sadnesses. I have also come to believe that it may be the most destructive emotion, for it is where the bond is destroyed and the masquerade begins.

Your experience of shame may not be bed-wetting, but perhaps it's from being bullied back in middle school or being mocked for wearing the "wrong" outfit to a party. Maybe you struggled with stuttering in class or poor coordination in sports. Perhaps you were so ashamed of your alcoholic father that you never invited friends over for fear of how he would

> For shame is primal, the first fallen emotion recorded in Scripture.

behave. Or maybe it was the darker disgrace of being sexually violated by someone you thought you could trust. It could be any number of things that call down the avalanche of shame. But whatever the cause, the experience of it is so crushing that you immediately cover and hide, vowing to do whatever it takes to avoid further shame.

Tragically, it is that same vow that gives shame its titanic power. We become self-protective. We become guarded. We are never as carefree again. And the voice of shame incessantly gnaws at us: "Run. Hide. Never tell anyone. Protect your secret. If you ever tell, it will only mean more shame." The running shapes our personalities, our careers, our marriages, our families, even our view of God. But there is one thing shame can never do. It can never drive us to bond.

The Unmasking Begins

The New Testament language for the horizontal bond among believers is cast in the "one another" appeals. We are instructed to submit to one another, serve one another, honor one another, forgive one another, love one another, and so on. But there is one particular appeal that may give us the clearest entrance into the bond: "Therefore, confess your sins to one another and pray for one another, so that you may be healed" (James 5:16). If just this one verse were intentionally pursued, I believe it would be the cause for deep revival. But there is a cost. The running must stop.

I remember backpacking with some young men several years ago. The sun was out, but it was a cool November day. We came to a waterfall that spilled into a small swimming hole. The challenge was given: "Who's going to get in?" After much hemming and hawing, two of them stripped down and slowly lowered themselves into the freezing water. They hurriedly swam to the other side and then back, screaming and laughing. After drying off, they felt invigorated, both by the water and by their feat. But I couldn't bring myself to do it and regretted my reluctance the rest of the day. So the next time I had the chance at another swimming hole on another backpacking trip, my decision was already made. I remember sticking my foot in the frigid water and wondering if my heart was going to stop. I gingerly lowered myself in, swam to the other side, and then quickly circled back. As I pulled myself out onto the rocks, it felt as if my skin had grown new nerve endings. Everything was tingling, alive.

> If James 5:16 were intentionally pursued, I believe it would be the cause for deep revival. But there is a cost. The running must stop.

Something like this is what we feel when we begin to confess our sins. Honestly, it feels like we are going to die, like our heart is going to stop. We avoid it, like I did that first chance to swim, and then we finally get up the courage to jump in. We brace ourselves for the worst, but what we discover is the opposite. We come out feeling invigorated and alive. Something has shifted. We've stopped hiding from God. Now we've stopped hiding from others.

In the story groups I lead, men learn to tell their story with an honesty few of them have ever experienced. The first meeting always begins with awkwardness and some fear. I can see the look in their eyes. They are getting ready to jump into ice-cold water. The shame, the sin, the sadness . . . it will all come out in the light. But what we experience by the last meeting is entirely the opposite—invigoration, newness, life. We have seen each other's hearts unveiled, aching and alive. We have begun to bond.

Walking with Others

But the best way to feel the bond may be the simplest: walking intimately with a few friends. This has been my experience with two close friends, Matt and Bruce. Some time ago, I suggested we read a book together and begin a conversation about our lives. I needed it desperately. The conversation started with our stories and personal struggles and moved on into our marriages, our families, and our dreams. And then our deeper fears came out onto the table. One morning I admitted to them my fear of rejection, that telling my story would cause them to despise me. Bruce then admitted his fear that he had nothing substantial to offer, that he was just a country boy and not very special. Matt admitted his fear of going back into the lonely black holes where he has lived for much of his life.

> It is simply to talk about our hearts, what we are battling through, what God is teaching us, where we need help.

With that conversation, the unmasking had really begun. Now when we meet weekly, it is simply to talk about our hearts, what we are battling through, what God is teaching us, and where we need help. Often the hour passes, and we feel we have just begun.

But there has been yet another important shift that has come with the unmasking. One summer, Bruce went through a painful situation where doing the right thing cost him dearly. One Sunday after church, he was particularly hurting and saw me walking nearby. He came over with tears in his eyes, confiding that he didn't need answers but just needed me to be there with him. I remember feeling surprised by my impact on him. On another occasion, Bruce and I both expressed to Matt that we feel safe when he is leading the way. He conveys a quiet strength that we have both learned to trust. Matt's response was similar to mine—surprise. And when Bruce taught me to duck hunt one winter, I told him how much it meant to me, that I needed men like him to mentor me. Bruce received it, but again, with some surprise and even reluctance.

What was happening to us is the shift that comes with all true bonding. We were learning the impact we were having on each other. We were learning to feel what others felt toward us. This is exactly what I had been learning with the Father in my attempts to bond with Him. I was learning to feel what He felt about me as His son, not only that He delights in me but that my life impacts His, that my presence and love affect Him.

And now this landmark has ushered us into strange and enchanting terrain, a land full of wonder and light. This is where the bond begins to take us, a bond that can never be severed, not even by death. But there is one more significant bond we have yet to explore.

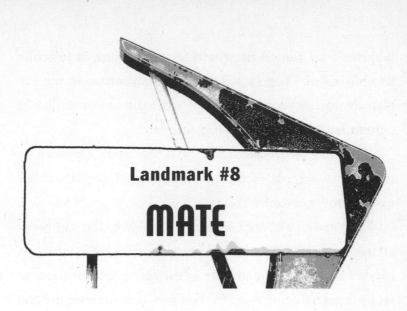

Landmark #8

MATE

When I have learnt to love God better than my earthly dearest,
I shall love my earthly dearest better than I do now.

—C. S. Lewis

The growth of love is not a straight line,
but a series of hills and valleys.

—Madeleine L'Engle

Julie sat behind me in the fourth grade. I hardly noticed her on most days, but there were moments when I did. Sometimes our teacher would give out papers to the kids in the front desks so that they could hand them out to those in their row. I was in that front position, so after taking my own paper, I would turn around and give the rest to Julie. I don't remember having any conversation with her, but I do remember that I loved to look at her. She was beautiful. There was a gentle radiance that seemed to glow from her face and mingle with the shimmer in her golden hair. I just wanted to gaze.

That day desire awoke in me. I was being summoned out of my boyish world by something I could neither understand nor verbalize.

Of course, I did not know how to answer the summons at age ten. No one does. But I heard it again five years later. My life had changed radically as the safe world of elementary school had given way to the fears of middle school and the perils of high school. I felt alone and afraid for much of the school day, but I had also met Jesus during that time, and He kept me hopeful and alive. If I couldn't trust my peers at school, at least I could trust Him. And then, the summer before my sophomore year, I met Margaret.

> I was being summoned out of my boyish world by something I could neither understand nor verbalize.

She had also encountered Jesus in a way that had changed the trajectory of her life. We met at the church youth group I had started to attend that summer. I felt accepted by everyone there, but it was Margaret who captivated me. One evening after the youth meeting, one of the college-age leaders offered to take some of us out for ice cream in his Ford Mustang convertible. I remember sitting in the back seat with Margaret, watching her hair blow in the warm breeze. I felt the call of beauty again. But this time there was more to the summons.

Margaret had touched the deep sadness of my disconnection by showing interest in me. Whenever we would talk, I felt heard. I felt safe. I especially remember one summer afternoon before the weekly meeting when we found ourselves outside on the church grounds. The beaming of the sun matched the light I felt radiating from my own heart. We sat on soft, freshly mown grass conversing and laughing as we gently teased each another. I felt excited, haunted by an allure I could not control. Nor did I want to. This time, the summons was not just about beauty but about the intimacy that came with it. I tasted the beauty of a woman's heart for the first time, and I was hooked. I had never dated a girl before, but I wanted to with Margaret.

But that never happened. I found out through some mutual friends that she was already going out with someone else. And this was no ordinary someone else; he was the captain and quarterback of a well-known football team in the area. I was crushed. My own sense of manhood was teetering on the nonexistent anyway, and my poor showing in athletics seemed to push that feeling over the edge. So with such an imposing rival, I took what seemed to be the only possible course of action.

It happened one Sunday when Margaret brought him to church. He was descending the steps into the large hall where coffee and doughnuts were served after the service. I stood at the opposite end of the hall watching him from a distance. I remember seeing him and feeling a stabbing ache in my heart. This sensation was followed by a freezing tightness in my chest, as if I had plunged my heart into the Arctic Ocean. I turned and walked out, never to see him again and never to have any serious relationship with Margaret. Years later, I put these words to what I had decided in that moment: "If loving a girl feels like this, I will never love again." And I kept that promise for years. For I had answered the summons, and it had led to unimaginable pain. Desire had betrayed me, so I took my revenge on it and viciously buried it.

Desire Aroused

I tell this story because it gives a fitting view of the terrain for this landmark, a terrain jutted like razor-sharp peaks and deeply gutted canyons, where nothing is gentle or rolling, where everything can feel raw and dangerous. This is the terrain of desire for someone like us, yet different—the desire for a mate. It can erupt at unpredictable moments and insist on a response, moving us toward the opposite sex and eventually compelling us down the wedding aisle. Of course, none of us really has any idea what we are getting into with marriage. But desire beckons, and we feel constrained to follow.

Think of this desire as a rope made out of three strands. For a man, one strand depicts his need for love. He hopes to find a place where he can be fully known and understood, where he can be emotionally naked and unashamed. He longs to dismantle the protective walls and bask in the company of his beloved. This longing is intertwined with the second strand of sexual desire. Men carry the hope that the sexual struggles they have slogged through will be smoothed over after marriage. Perhaps they dream of sexual abandonment night after night. At the very least they hope that sexual temptation won't be so relentless or compelling. Finally, the third strand—the center around which the other two are wound—is the longing for beauty. This is aroused in the presence of a woman, yet not tied to any one woman.

A man can also feel the yearning for beauty when a vivid sunset appears on the horizon or when he stares in wonder at a mountain range. But beauty is incarnated in a woman. It does not have the physicality of sex or the emotional sway of love. Its pull is more subtle, like a whisper. Beauty is particularized in each woman in ways suiting her own texture and bent, but it is present in all women. And a man feels the pull. Beauty calls out to him, and he wants to enter and enjoy.

He is looking for woman.

The feminine side of this desire also has three strands. She too feels the ache for love and intimacy, but it runs stronger in her than in a man, like a river that narrows. The water has to run swifter now, and the pull of intimacy feels swifter in a woman, even wild and insatiable at times. Sexual desire is also there, but it is tied much tighter to the emotional arousal of being loved and desired. The two strands cannot be as easily fragmented as they can in men. And in the center of these is the woman's longing to be in the presence of strength, to be with someone she can respect and lean on. She wants to be partnered with someone who knows where he is going and is confident on getting them both there. She wants to enter in and rest.

> When a couple say their vows and exchange the rings, they are both to some degree banking on finding all that they have been longing for.

She is looking for man.

When a couple say their vows and exchange the rings, they are both to some degree banking on finding all that they have been longing for. Desire has issued the summons, and they have dropped everything to follow.

Desire Betrayed

But sooner or later the disappointments come. I know of one couple who, while on their honeymoon, began to wonder if they had made the biggest mistake of their lives. For Heidi, the unsettling feeling came very soon after our wedding. She not only wondered if this was all there was; she began to wonder if there was any way out. She had longed for a knight in shining armor to come and rescue her. Coming from a home where both parents were alcoholics, she felt trapped, just surviving the daily chaos. When I came along, she saw me as the escape to a new existence of freedom, away from the control of her father and the emptiness of her mother. But my own pain and disconnection had rendered me unable and often unwilling to enter the lives of others. This knight had gone back into the castle and pulled up the drawbridge. Heidi had exchanged the trap of control for the trap of aloneness. In our early years I remember her telling me through tears, "I feel so lonely in our marriage." I could hear her words, but I couldn't respond. Something inside me felt locked, inaccessible. Remember, my heart had been frozen in the Arctic Ocean.

On my side, the disappointment settled in sometime during our first year. I had married for many reasons, among them being drawn to Heidi's beauty and needing a partner in ministry. But she pulled back from helping me as her loneliness set in. She became increasingly hurt and angry. And with the anger, her beauty (to me) seemed to vaporize. I was left confused and fearful. What had I done? Had I made a terrible mistake? My terror and shame grew, and I responded in the only way I knew how. I locked the drawbridge and built the walls higher. Heidi was left more alone than ever.

In almost every marriage, something like this goes awry. No matter how good things may appear at first, the experience doesn't match the expectation. The arguments begin. The misunderstandings. The hurt. We feel confused. Then we feel betrayed. And the feeling of betrayal moves in even if our spouse never hints at an affair, for the betrayal stems from another source. We may conclude that it's God's fault, that He has betrayed us. But the real culprit is much closer to home. It's us. It's our hearts. Our own desires betrayed us.

How we respond to this betrayal now becomes the theme of so much of our married lives. We may wonder if finding another marriage will answer this desire. Or maybe we'll just preoccupy ourselves with the children or a career. Perhaps we'll turn to something more tangible, like the next paycheck or the next vacation or the next night out. Whatever we don't find in our marriage, we look for elsewhere, like a hungry animal scavenging for food.

We may even try to kill the desire simply by settling: *This is as good as it gets. I just need to get over the naiveté of love and romance and get on with life the best I can.* This is where so many marriages end up, just surviving. It's a functional marriage, and it may work to some degree. But this sounds more like the mechanical functioning of a tractor, not the wonder of two becoming one.

> In almost every marriage, something like this goes awry. No matter how good things may appear at first, the experience doesn't match the expectation.

And here the marriage runs aground. The "one" has fragmented back into two. Somehow we have missed God's design.

Why Our Marriages Don't Work

So why doesn't marriage work for so many? Why is desire betrayed, sometimes brutally? Revisiting the first five landmarks can help us find some clarity.

Each of us comes into marriage scripting some basic story for ourselves. That was the first landmark. There is some deeply gripped conviction that our lives must go a certain way. When two people begin to live together, each with different and often conflicting story lines, the attempted fusion easily moves to confusion and then collision. What's going to happen to a marriage when the man centers his story on always being right and the woman settles on being a survivor? What happens when a man who thinks he is on his own marries a woman who has vowed to disconnect to avoid further relational pain?

Think now of the second landmark—idols. When we write our own stories, they always include the God-substitutes we choose to help us maneuver through life. As long as we are still clinging to them, we can't be fully married to our spouse. Our idols are our lovers, our places of comfort and relief. So what happens when a man who drinks to control his anxiety marries a woman who must control everything, including him? What happens when the husband becomes married to his work or the wife becomes married to her children or vice versa?

Continue on to our wounds, the third landmark. We all carry them into our marriages, for we have all been sinned against. We are all damaged goods, as Heidi likes to say. So what happens when the angry man who winced under the abuse of his father marries a woman who was ignored by her own father? What happens in the marriage when either or both spouses were bullied by siblings or fellow students? Remember, wounded people wound people. And the wounds marital partners can now inflict on each other are frightening.

The fourth landmark spoke of sexual insanity, something that can easily invade any marriage. Here the pull of sexual desire runs amuck, fragmented from the other strands. Sex becomes mechanical or breaks out beyond the bonds of marriage. But remember that the core sadness in this landmark is that our sexuality is broken. A man aches for a woman, and a woman longs to be in the presence of a man. But these longings are continually disappointed because so many men are emasculated and so many women are disconnected from their core femininity. And when the two marry, they soon begin to drift apart, like astronauts who've gotten detached from their lifelines.

> A man aches for a woman, and a woman longs to be in the presence of a man. But these longings are continually disappointed because so many men are emasculated and so many women are disconnected from their core femininity.

Finally, we come to the landmark of identity, the deep beliefs that define us. How we see ourselves becomes pivotal in marriage. Again, imagine some of the possible scenarios. What happens when a man who deeply believes he is a failure marries a woman who is convinced she is unworthy of love? What happens when both of them are convinced that they must perform in some way to find affirmation?

Whatever our original hopes for marriage were, they often fade into settling, surviving, despairing, or looking for an exit. To push up and out of this tangled morass, something else has to happen, something extraordinary.

The Blessed Hope

Something extraordinary can happen, but only if we let go. We have to let go of writing the story of our own marriage, for it's not really about our own marriage anyway. It's about the story God is telling and the story He wants to tell through our marriages. That's the realm of the extraordinary.

The tenor of the New Testament is not *Use the grace that Jesus gives and receive the greatest gift of all, a wonderful marriage.* It just doesn't fly in that direction. But I believe it is often subtly communicated this way, that marriage is the *summum bonum*, the greatest possible good in life. And when marriage becomes the supreme good, we are in for trouble. For if marriage is the chief end of man, what happens to those who are too young to be married, or to those who have never been married, or to those whose spouse has died? What about those who have been deserted by their spouse or those who are married to someone deeply troubled?

> We have to let go of writing the story of our own marriage, for it's not really about our own marriage anyway.

Here we find ourselves hitting up against a wall of Scripture. Paul himself was single, at least during his ministry, and he even promoted the advantages of being

156

single: "Are you married? Do not seek a divorce. Are you unmarried? Do not look for a wife. But if you do marry, you have not sinned; and if a virgin marries, she has not sinned. But those who marry will face many troubles in this life, and I want to spare you this" (1 Cor. 7:27–28 NIV). How could singleness be so great if marriage is the greatest good? Perhaps we need a paradigm shift.

And here is the shift. The tenor of the New Testament is much more like this: *The greatest gift has been given to you, the redemption that Jesus labored to bring about. He is making everything new and will complete the job when He returns. This is the great hope that you can count on even if everything else fails you in this life. For what He is doing will never fail.* This is the realm of the extraordinary. This is the story God is writing. This is the blessed hope.

Part of this redemption can happen in marriage as a subset of the deep work of Jesus, a room He is cleaning out and setting in order (a large room to be sure, but certainly not the whole house). For whatever our marital status or state of our marriage, in some sense it really doesn't matter. We can choose to enter the extraordinary. We can enter the great Story and

> We can enter the great Story and follow the landmarks whether our spouse comes or not, or whether we even have a spouse.

follow the landmarks whether our spouse comes or not, whether we even have a spouse.

For the blessed hope is not a great marriage. The blessed hope is that Jesus "will wipe every tear from their eyes. Death will no longer exist; grief, crying, and pain will exist no longer, because the previous things have passed away" (Rev. 21:4). When I let go and set my deepest hope there, I have the freedom to enjoy the good things I am given here, including my marriage, without placing the full weight of my longings on them. For He is making everything beautiful and new. And that involves turning us into creatures of radiant strength and beauty, starting now. But the journey there can take us through some painful territory.

A Painful Conversation

I have already mentioned how our marriage began. The next stage of it was characterized by a tense truce between us. We were both very busy, as Heidi filled her days with mothering and I filled mine with teaching and coaching. But the truce would sometimes fall apart over some minor misunderstanding. The disagreement would then elicit angry or sullen responses all out of proportion to the issue at hand. We were both tinderboxes of emotion.

One of the most painful conversations we ever had took place during this time. Over a spring break, we were given the use of a cabin on a nearby lake and went as a family for what we hoped would be a few days of recovery and rest. One day, while both daughters were napping, Heidi and I went for a walk. The conversation quickly moved from the mundane into the muddle of our lives. I don't remember the exact words we spoke to each other, but we broached the dark emotion that lay beneath the surface. I remember feeling raw and exposed as the walk ended. I realized that I had often been playing a more feminine part, responding instead of initiating, waiting instead of leading. Heidi realized that she had taken up more of a masculine role, not because she wanted to but because she had to. She felt that she had to make the tough decisions or say the difficult things to the children. As she grew angrier over the role she felt cast in, I pulled back, in fear of her anger. The cycle continued until it had become a death spiral. For whatever reason, on that day I saw clearly what I had become, and I was disgusted with it. I desperately wanted to become a true

> I wanted to pull out of the death spiral. But how?

man, and somehow I knew that this was also the only way that Heidi would ever have the chance to become a true woman. I wanted to pull out of the death spiral. But how?

The answer soon came with an opportunity to attend a marital prayer retreat—five days filled with quiet reading, prayer walks, gourmet food, and counseling from an amazing couple. The breakthrough came for me halfway through the retreat. I remember walking through the picturesque fields while praying through some of the issues that had come up. I heard the Father speak to me five words, this time not in a quiet whisper but in an amplified voice that reverberated through my whole being. The words were simply this: "I want to heal you." And the healing wasn't just about the idols and wounds from my past. For the extraordinary goes beyond the undoing of evil. It's about taking the muddle of our lives and turning it into something dazzling. For me, the healing meant the prospect of being resurrected as a man.

Since that pivotal moment, I began to get much more clarity about the landmarks and made significant motion toward them. For her part, Heidi no longer felt she always had to prop me up or hold things together. She now had the emotional energy to attend to her own soul as a woman, to move toward her own fears and into the presence of the Father who could release her from them. What Heidi and I began to experience is what this landmark is all about. It's not an action plan to a good marriage. It's about becoming a person with whom an extraordinary marriage is possible. It's about becoming extraordinary men and women.

Becoming Solid, Becoming Secure

The Hebrew word for *glory* carries the idea of being heavy or weighty. The point is that God's glory is of such substance and density that His presence becomes impossible to dismiss or ignore. Paul states that we have all fallen short of this glory (Rom. 3:23), that we have all missed the mark and thus missed being connected to God's glory. As a result, our lives have lost a sense of significance and radiance. We've become both flimsy and fogged. For a man, this means that he has become vacuous, lacking density at his very core. So much of his endless chasing is an unconscious compulsion to find solidity. But the only way to find it is to go back to the source of glory.

Later in the book of Romans, Paul says that with the peace that comes through justification, we can now "rejoice in the hope of the glory of God" (5:2). This is not just the hope of worshipping God for His glory. This is also the hope that a man will be pierced and illuminated by that glory so that he can become fully man. And that hope is not just for heaven. It begins now. When a man moves through the landmarks, he begins to taste his solidity. He will begin to feel his manhood bestowed on him by the Father and can then offer it to a woman. He becomes a man who cannot be dismissed or ignored, who does not demand things from a woman but instead invites her into the life he is experiencing.

What then happens to a woman when she begins to share in the glory of God? Here, I can no longer speak from personal experience, but from listening to women, reading about them, and living with one for many years. When a woman begins to connect to God's glory, she becomes secure. In that security, she feels loved, not for what she can do or offer, but simply because she is a woman. She feels delighted in for her very being, and when a woman feels this type of delight and enjoyment from the living God, she begins to radiate out from her truest self, a luminosity filled with both beauty and mystery. As a man's true strength must be called out by an affirmation outside of him, so a woman's true beauty must be kindled by a love exterior to her. And this is exactly what connecting to God's glory does. Instead of the frantic search for affection or the compulsive cry for attention, there is rest in her soul. And in that rest comes the courage to offer what is most deeply hers, in the hope that others will find it life-giving.

Not long ago, Heidi met me in the kitchen as I came home from school. She had spent the morning with a younger woman who needed support and counsel in her own marital difficulties. After briefly telling me about the time, Heidi came over to me, put her arms around me, and softly told me how thankful she was to be married to me. I was caught off guard by her lightness and openness. This was not the usual chitchat we exchange after a day of work, and I struggled in the moment to open myself and receive her thankfulness. But the next morning as I began to journal, I reflected on how different our marriage had become, how different I was feeling, and how much terrain Heidi and I had covered. We were entering the realm of the extraordinary. And what lies before us now is the last landmark, one we can walk toward together.

> As a man's true strength must be called out by an affirmation outside of him, so a woman's true beauty must be kindled by a love exterior to her.

Landmark #9

QUEST

This quest may be attempted by the weak with as much hope as the strong. Yet it is oft the course of deeds that move the wheels of the world: Small hands do them because they must, while the eyes of the great are elsewhere.

—J. R. R. TOLKIEN

If you want to identify me, ask me not where I live, or what I like to eat, or how I comb my hair, but ask me what I am living for, in detail, ask me what I think is keeping me from living fully for the thing I want to live for.

—THOMAS MERTON

I like to think of myself as someone who loves an adventure. Until I actually go on one. Then I'm not so sure.

Several summers ago, I was invited by a good friend and colleague to take some students salmon fishing in

Alaska. I was intrigued by the idea for I had pored over maps of Alaska for years wondering what it would be like to go there. My intrigue quickly turned to decision. I would go on this adventure.

The journey started tamely enough. The preparations and flight all went according to plan as did the drive north from Anchorage to our campsite. But the trip turned sour when our first two days of fishing brought hours of fly-tying and casting, but no fish. Instead of grilled salmon, we ate chicken and potatoes for dinner the first night, then just potatoes the second. But we were determined to find the salmon, and that meant another turn in the adventure.

Next to our campsite was a place where we could rent rafts that would take us down the nearby Little Willow River. Our idea was to go farther down the river where we could meet the salmon coming in late for their upstream spawning. With visions of floating down a gentle stream, I pictured this to be a fun and relaxing day. The man in charge of the rentals drove us to the put-in site, unloaded the rafts, and hastily instructed us on how to steer them with oars. As he left us, I walked over to take my first real look at the river. This was no lazy, meandering stream, but a tight, rapid waterway that seemed to require super-human skill to navigate. Fear rose up in me, tightening my chest. What had I gotten myself into?

We soon launched onto the river, ill-prepared for what was about to happen next. It immediately propelled us toward a tight bend where a large felled tree stuck halfway out into the current. We slammed right into it, but somehow maneuvered our way around the jabbing branches, extricating ourselves from the tangle. The next raft was not so lucky. It too crashed into the tree but completely flipped over, sending two of the young men down into a hydraulic hole. Panic set in as they frantically tried to force themselves up and out of the water. A minute later, everyone was safe, except for a 12-gauge shotgun lost forever in the current. If there had ever been any doubt about the power of this river, it quickly vanished. We all became wary. You could tell it by the edge in our voices. *Could we pull this off?* I began to wonder if coming to Alaska was a huge mistake, if coming to this river was an even bigger one. But there was only one way to go now—forward.

So on we went, and after some time of banging into branches and scraping against rocks, we began to get the hang of steering the rafts. We took a break to eat lunch, got out onto the shoreline, and finally caught our first fish, some rainbow trout. Still no salmon, but we felt better after catching something. We returned to the rafts and floated down another section of the Little Willow until it joined the broad Susitna River. We were greeted there by a sheer expanse of glacial-fed water and exquisite yellow and purple blossoms decorating the shoreline. What was left of apprehension soon gave way to wonder. We were awed by a rugged beauty that no photo could ever capture. That night, after coming off the river, we sat around a crackling campfire, enjoying the aroma of sizzling trout and talking about our fears and feats of the day. Even though we had failed to find salmon again, we had no regrets about the rafting venture. We had stared down the perils and unknowns and had come out as better men. Our sense of satisfaction only deepened when we found salmon by the hundreds the very next day.

But in my Alaskan quest pales in comparison to one I once read about, the Lewis and Clark expedition. These two men, along with their crew, oared upstream for months to find the source of the Missouri River and hopefully a waterway across America to the Pacific. They had only a few roughly sketched maps for the first part of the journey and then had to rely on the help of the Hidatsa Indians to find the headwaters of the Missouri. Fortunately, they found a sure-footed Shoshone guide to accompany them for the next leg of the journey, a perilous trip over the Rockies. After two years they finally reached the Pacific, only to have to turn around and do it all over again for the return home. They really had no idea what they were getting into when they started out on the expedition. But it seemed their destiny to take up this quest. It was the dream branded on their hearts, and along the way they became determined to finish or die in the attempt.

We often read adventure stories like this as an escape hatch. Our day-to-day grind feels so different. Living a destiny? We tend to settle and manage. Determined to finish or die? We clock in and out for the day. And what about the dreams once branded on our hearts? We often find them evaporating in the harsh glare of reality. This is the quandary we find ourselves in as we approach the last landmark—the quest. And what happens in this quandary is all too familiar: we smother the longing, or it gets smothered with busyness.

> We often read adventure stories like this as an escape. Our day-to-day grind feels so different.

The Quest in Stories

Yet despite our best efforts, the longing for a quest never quite leaves us, erupting at unforeseen moments. It may happen when we watch a movie where someone chooses to do the right thing even when it is costly. Or it may occur when we read a novel where the main character decides to leave the familiar behind and step out into the perilous to follow a passion. Something in us fires and smolders long after the movie credits have rolled and the book is closed. At some level, we all ache to live this way even when our usual posture is to play it safe. Our submerged longing has suddenly connected with a story, and with good reason. The quest forms the structure of nearly every novel written and every movie filmed.

Every story is shaped around a main character who is asked to go on a journey to find something, get something, or become something. This is his quest. And along the way he confronts major obstacles. Some of them are external enemies, often focused in a single adversary, while others are internal character flaws he becomes aware of as he moves forward. He must figure out how to maneuver around all of these hindrances to keep the quest alive. Often he experiences defeat, yet he gets up and keeps going. And in the end, if the story has a happy ending, he succeeds in the quest. He obtains what he went for, and in the process finds out who he really is.

> The quest forms the structure of nearly every novel written and every movie filmed.

A few examples may help clarify the point. In Shakespeare's stirring *Henry V*, King Henry goes on a quest to conquer lands from France that he feels are rightly his. In *Les Miserables*, Jean Valjean, a former prisoner, receives a small fortune from a priest and goes on a quest to redeem his life and spread goodness. *Grapes of Wrath* is the quest of a farm-tenant family trying to survive the

Dust Bowl era of the 1930s. *The Matrix* highlights the quest of Neo, who must learn to fight the enemy agents so that he can release the human race from bondage. And the fairy tale *Beauty and the Beast* recounts the quest of a prince-turned-beast who must learn to love a woman and cause her to love him in return before the spell is broken.

I think the art of storytelling here is in some way reflective of reality. It's trying to tell us something about our hearts. The quest is not just something we are to read or watch. It's something we are to enter.

Our lives are supposed to be a quest.

The Quest in the Bible

Skepticism about such a quixotic statement is certainly understandable. "You can't possibly mean that. These are just stories created for our entertainment. How could our lives ever look like that?" Good question. But the possibility of a quest gathers momentum and presses in dangerously close when we open the pages of the great Story itself, the Bible. Here we find God intersecting the lives of fallen men and women and what happens then looks strongly familiar. He calls them out on a quest.

The foundational quest is given to Abraham in Genesis. God asks him to leave behind everything significant to him—his home, his community, and his gods—and then gives him a task: go and find the land I will show you. Abraham has no idea what he is getting himself into when he packs up and leaves. But the next thirteen chapters of Genesis show us enough mistakes, defeats, and unforeseen obstacles to make a classic action film.

Moses begins his quest when he meets the Lord unexpectedly in a fiery bush in the middle of the Sinai desert. The task he is given? Take God's people out of Egypt and lead them into the land of promise. After making initial excuses, Moses takes up the harrowing quest, leading a vast throng through the desert with little preparation or provision.

> Here we find God intersecting the lives of fallen men and women and what happens then looks strongly familiar. He calls them out on a quest.

Gideon is called to take up the quest of delivering his people from the hand of the Midianites. The angel of the Lord addresses him as "mighty warrior." I imagine Gideon was at first convinced the angel must have confused him with someone else. But he decides to go and fight anyway even with his fear and uncertainty. And with the Lord's personal coaching, he routs the Midianites in battle.

Nehemiah's quest starts with tears and longing, for his beloved city Jerusalem is in ruins. The longing elicits prayer, and God answers by opening the doors for his quest to begin, the rebuilding of Jerusalem's walls. Along the way, he confronts ridicule, slander, and plots on his life. But in the end the walls are rebuilt, and the people's hearts are rekindled.

Isaiah listens intently to God's question, "Whom shall I send? Who will go for us?" He answers in the affirmative even before he knows the details of his quest. All he knows is that God's holiness and grace have seared his heart. The mission? Be God's spokesman. The message? Judgment is coming on Israel. As a postscript, he is informed that his message is only going to harden the people's hearts, but he must speak it anyway.

Jeremiah had a similar calling at an earlier age. Imagine being sixteen and told you are to go and speak to world leaders. And with the command comes an ominous warning: you will be opposed and ridiculed all along the way.

The New Testament holds to the same pattern. Jesus calls the disciples to drop everything and follow Him. But they misunderstand the quest from the beginning. They dream of holding positions of power as the inner ring around Israel's new king. Instead, Jesus calls them to be eyewitnesses of His resurrection life, a message they are to spread throughout the world. As a result, most of them end up facing martyrdom.

We can't leave out the apostle Paul. On the road to Damascus, he is ambushed by Jesus, causing him to abandon his previous quest to stamp out Christianity. His new assignment? Be the primary spokesman for Jesus' work to the entire non-Jewish world. His quest takes him on four missionary journeys, two imprisonments and enough obstacles to make it all appear impossible at times. But Paul is given enough passion to push through, and the impossible happens.

The pattern is too obvious to ignore. God's call becomes the quest. And the quest becomes the story. And the story becomes the message. We can write these stories off as unique or label them as "Bizarre and Impractical Bible Stories Definitely Not for Today." But there's a problem. The same Bible clearly states that Jesus is the same yesterday as He is today. And there is not one whiff of evidence that He has stopped calling out men and women on a quest. Here are two real-life stories.

> The Bible clearly states that Jesus is the same yesterday as He is today.

The Quest for Patrick and Myrtie

Patrick's quest is one of the great missionary tales of church history. He lived from the late 300s AD into the 400s, but we still know of him today through the holiday that bears his name, St. Patrick's Day. What we often don't know is the story of his quest.

Patrick was born in Roman Britain. Calpornius, his father, was a deacon in the church, and his grandfather, Potitus, was a priest. When Patrick was about sixteen, he was captured and carried off to Ireland as a slave, where he worked as a herdsman. During that captivity, his faith in Jesus grew, and he prayed daily. After six years he heard a voice telling him that he would soon return home, and then another voice informed him that his ship was ready. He fled his captor, found the ship, and made his way back to England, only to come to the brink of death with the ship's crew as they traveled across uninhabited land. Nearing starvation, Patrick confidently prayed, and a herd of swine soon appeared, saving many of them from death. He eventually made it back to his hometown where we pick up the story in his own words from his *Confession*:

> And after a few years I was again in Britain with my parents [kinsfolk], and they welcomed me as a son, and asked me, in faith, that after the great tribulations I had endured I should not go anywhere else away from them. And, of course, there, in a vision of the night, I saw a man whose name was Victoricus coming as if from Ireland with innumerable letters, and he gave me one of them, and I read the beginning of the letter: "The Voice of the Irish"; and as I was reading the beginning of the letter I seemed at that moment to hear the

voice of those who were beside the forest of Foclut which is near the western sea, and they were crying as if with one voice: "We beg you, holy youth, that you shall come and shall walk again among us." And I was stung intensely in my heart so that I could read no more, and thus I awoke.

Patrick obeyed the voice. Against his family's wishes, he went back to the place where he had been taken by force, no longer as a slave, but as a missionary. Because of his courage and obedience, his life was transformed, and so was Ireland. He succeeded in baptizing thousands of converts from Druidic paganism, including kings and their families.

Myrtie Howard was also called out on a quest. But instead of in the fourth century AD, hers came in the 1960s. Instead of a young Anglo man in his twenties, she was an elderly black woman in her seventies. Instead of being released from captivity to go on a quest, this woman was placed in captivity for her quest, confined to a wheelchair in a nursing home. And instead of the worldwide fame of Patrick, Myrtie lived in relative obscurity.

She was born into very poor surroundings in Texas, worked in the local mill as a child, married at seventeen, and was widowed in her forties. She then lived through the death of her youngest son and struggled with her own declining health. Forced to move into a nursing home, she began to feel the downward pull of depression. One day she simply told the Lord she was ready to die unless He had something else for her to do. In response, she heard three words: "Write to prisoners." Her quest had come.

Excuses immediately appeared in her mind. She had no formal education and had to teach herself to read and write. More importantly, she knew nothing about prisons or prisoners. But being a woman of faith and obedience, she wrote to the local penitentiary, asking that any prisoners who desired friendship write her back. Eight of them responded. That number eventually grew until she had corresponded over time with hundreds. Her game plan? "When I get a letter, I read it, and when I answer it, I pray: 'Lord, You know what You want me to say. Now say it through me.' And you'd be surprised sometimes at the letters He writes!"

The letters she received from prisoners were often brimming with thankfulness and love for this obscure, elderly woman. They were only matched by the radiant joy on her face. Her response sums it up well: "I've had the greatest time of my life since I've been writing to prisoners."

What Happens When Life Becomes a Quest

But life without a quest becomes a very different story. Here we try to avoid pain, minimize risk, and grab at anything that will give us a momentary lift. Yet this only ends up pulling us into a centripetal path. Centripetal forces are those that pull toward a center, as a satellite is pulled into orbit by the earth's gravity. In the same way, our idols cause us to pull into ourselves, making us believe that everything is about us, forcing us to warp all of reality around the constraints of our fears and addictions. Into this sucking black hole, everyone around us feels the pull. And it's not life-giving. It's a death pull.

By contrast, quests are centrifugal, forces that push us outward. You may remember the feeling of playing whiplash on skates. If you were the last one in a line of circling skaters, you felt the strong pull to be flung out, away from the other skaters. Quests are like that. They fling us outward, expanding our hearts. Life is not just about us anymore. It's about the quest. We become aware as never before of those around us, alive to what they need, what they feel.

> Life is not just about us anymore. It's about the quest.

To live the quest also requires that we offer something from our deepest, truest self. This is why I have positioned this landmark as the last one. We are living closer to the light of the Father now, and the reflection we offer to others is crisper, sharper, and more focused. The quest is not something tacked on to us, like another chore to perform or another attempt to gain affirmation. The quest is a passion, a deep welling up of something inside of us that feels fierce and unmanageable. The quest asks that we live out of our core, doing what we know we *must* do with our lives, not clawing for the approval of others.

But to take a quest is risky business, often taking us straight into our deepest fears. We must now turn and face them if we are serious about the quest. In God's good and odd providence, this is how He fathers us so that we can be released from those fears. Of course, we are never asked to face them alone. He will walk with us every step of the way.

Finally, the quest is about completing the work, finishing the task, crossing the finish line. We may come in limping, bleeding, with sweat pouring down, with tears blinding our eyes. But it's not about success or failure anymore. It's about doing the deed. It's about fulfilling the mission. And in the end, as with all good quests, we not only do the thing asked of us, we find ourselves doing things that we could have never imagined possible.

> We not only do the thing asked of us, we find ourselves doing things that we could have never imagined possible.

Taking the Inner Quest

The question may now be surfacing: "What then is my quest?" Some of you may already know, while others may have some vague sense about it. For the rest of you who have no idea, I certainly don't have all the answers, but I can tell you one place to start. You start with an inner quest.

Paul says that we are all "predestined to be conformed to the image of His Son, so that He would be the first-born among many brothers" (Rom. 8:29). We are to be chiseled into the image of the One who took the wildest and riskiest quest of all, dying for the sins of the whole world. He calls us now to follow His lead, for He knows all about quests and wants to direct us in ours so that we can become like Him.

But to become like Jesus here requires a prior quest, an inner quest, as epic and dangerous as any outward one I have ever known. Yet this inner quest is not another landmark, but the sum total of the first eight landmarks. They map out the inner quest and become the preparation, the training ground for the outer quest. For if the inner quest doesn't come first, we may not be able to hear the call when it comes; or if we do hear it, we may not be interested. Even if we choose the quest at this point, it will likely take the form of just another attempt at scripting our own story. My own experience bears this out.

Several years ago, I invited a guest speaker to the Sunday school class I teach. Through a miscommunication, I thought he was going to speak for fifteen minutes. Instead, he took the whole time. I enjoyed his presentation, but I walked out frustrated, as if I had geared up to run a race and had it cancelled at the last minute. It didn't help that I was also approaching a transition, uncertain of my life's direction at the time. I vented my frustration to the Father after church as I looked up to the sky, crying inwardly, *What am I supposed to do with all of this?*

> If the inner quest doesn't come first, we may not be able to hear the call when it comes; or if we do hear it, we may not be interested.

I got an unexpected reply: "Write."

I remember thinking at the time, *That was really odd.* But with the encouragement of two friends, an author and an editor, I decided to write out all of the lessons for my class. I then wrote up a book proposal and submitted it. The response? Rejection. I tried a second time with a different proposal. Same result. The third attempt yielded a little interest, but still no acceptance. I was frustrated and confused. Around this time, I was visiting a friend in

Colorado who was a published author. The morning after our time together, I awoke with something tugging at my heart. As I journaled and prayed in the fresh mountain air, I soon realized that the pull was one of the old lies I had listened to since early adolescence—that my path to happiness lay in having someone else's gifts or in trying to duplicate them. The lie was further empowered by another familiar feeling, a deep discontentment with myself. But as I journaled, I realized there was more.

I have always wanted to do something noteworthy, something significant. To be honest, I have always wanted to be famous. I know theoretically that it doesn't satisfy, that so many famous people are profoundly sad, but my heart still yearned for it anyway. It was the motivation behind many of my own self-constructed quests over the years. The longing for a name had now combined with the jealousy I felt toward someone who had a name, my author friend. My heart felt trapped, stuck in a prison I couldn't escape. In my desperation, I called out to the Father. Suddenly I remembered my past studies in Genesis.

In chapter 11, mankind got together to build the Tower of Babel, and the text says that they did it to "make a name" for themselves (Gen. 11:4), an idea that God opposed and eventually frustrated. By contrast, when Abraham was called out on his quest, God made a promise to him: "I will make your name great, and you will be a blessing" (Gen. 12:2). The point was clear. If I tried to achieve fame the fallen way, it would destroy me. But if I trusted God with my name, He would make it great, perhaps not in terms of the public eye, but great in His eyes and in the blessing it would give to others. I then realized that what my heart really ached for was recognition and applause, not from others but from my heavenly Father. And I had that fame already before him, even if I never got published.

> But God knows we desire to be significant, for He created us that way. What we don't realize is that our deepest significance is the effect we have on Him.

I tell this story because I had to cross that line in preparation as an author. I had to take the inner quest first; otherwise, writing would have become more of the same story I had lived in for years—self-hatred, jealousy, and a conniving scheme to find fame. But God knows our ache to be famous. He knows we desire to be significant, for He created us that way. What we don't realize is that our deepest significance is the effect we have on Him. Our truest fame is the fame we have before Him. So when we take up our quest, it may lead to renown or obscurity, but it doesn't really matter anymore. Our longing for quest has connected to the story God is weaving. That's all that matters.

The Quest and the Story

The apostle Paul authored some of the most classic quest statements in the Bible. As he was preparing to leave the church at Ephesus, he put these words to his quest longing: "But, I count my life of no value to myself, so that I may finish my course and the ministry I received from the Lord Jesus, to testify to the gospel of God's grace" (Acts 20:24). Near the end of his life, he penned this poignant disclosure to Timothy: "I have fought the good fight, I have finished the race, I have kept the faith" (2 Tim. 4:7). He knew he had fought his last battle, and he was ready to die and go home.

Paul also knew that his life was not an exception, but an example. Accordingly, he encouraged the church at Philippi this way: "Join with others in following my example" (Phil. 3:17 NIV). And to the Corinthians he urged, "Imitate me, as I also imitate Christ" (1 Cor. 11:1).

But how can *we* follow Paul's example? His role was unique in history. As the appointed ambassador to the Gentile world, he took the message of forgiveness in Jesus to the nations beyond Israel. He understood his own special role in God's story. He knew how his quest connected to it. But that's the whole point. Each of us also has something we need to do with our lives that no one else can do in quite the same way. We too have a unique role in the story of God's expanding kingdom. It will involve something we love to do and will draw on our individual gifts and strengths. But more than anything else, it will be what we were created to do, our own special line in the play He is writing. We must find that role, whatever it takes, however long it takes, and then do it. Otherwise something precious and irreplaceable will be lost. So much in our own lives depends on this. So much in the lives of those around us depends on this.

And now, as we come to the end of this last landmark, we discover that it arcs all the way back to the first one. For the quest is about finding our place in God's story. These two landmarks bookend the whole journey, moving us ever closer to the shores our true home, to heaven where the story will continue on. But we are not there. Not yet. We must now take whatever step is in front of us.

> We must find that role, whatever it takes, however long it takes, and then do it. Otherwise something precious and irreplaceable will be lost.

My Own Sense of the Quest

It is a perilous matter to talk about such things, much less write about them. For the step in front of me now feels much more like jumping off a cliff. After leaving the pastoral ministry many years ago, I took a job as a high school Bible teacher in a Christian school. I told everyone this would only be a one-year intermission, and then I would return to the ministry. But I soon came to realize that my quest lay there, that I was to take the truths of the Bible and find a way to connect them to the hearts of students. It was the adventure laid out before me, one that would last for twenty years.

But all of that is changing now. For during those twenty years, I have also been on an inner quest, fighting through all that assaulted me in my early years, all that nearly took me out. Along the way I became aware of the landmarks written about here. And now that has opened up a new quest—to get the landmarks out to others. But to do this, I have had to let go of my long-held role as a high school teacher. I will be leaving many things behind, including the familiarity of the classroom and the joy I have had teaching and coaching many young men and women. But a deeper joy beckons. I have never felt more unsure about my future, and never more exhilarated.

Some at my age are already thinking about retiring. I think I'm just beginning.

CONCLUSION

I love the recklessness of faith. First you leap,
and then you grow wings.

—WILLIAM SLOANE COFFIN JR.

My goal is to know [Christ] and the power of
His resurrection and the fellowship of His sufferings,
being conformed to His death, assuming that I will,
somehow reach the resurrection from among the dead.

—PHILIPPIANS 3:10–11

Recently two good friends kidnapped me one Saturday morning to take on the unthinkable—skydiving. One of them informed me that I had once mentioned my interest in trying it, and now they were just taking me up on my statement. Of course I don't remember saying any such thing, but I was not about to back down now, so in my most confident tone I announced that I was ready to go and jump with them. But underneath, I was jittery, shaky.

To add to my anxiety, the jump kept getting delayed, first by the sheer number of jumpers, then by an electrical outage, and finally by the weather. When the plane finally took off, we had been waiting for five long hours. After we ascended and leveled off at fourteen thousand feet, the Plexiglas door in the plane's side was thrust upward. The expert I was jumping with then instructed me to kneel at the very edge of the plane and then gave me a final countdown. As the cold air screamed past me, he tilted my head back on his shoulder and pushed me out into the void.

There was no previous category in my mind for what happened next. We turned a somersault in the air together, going from 0 to 120 mph in less than ten seconds. It is the closest parallel I have now to what death may feel like. I just had to let go and let myself fall. But once we reached terminal velocity at 120 mph, I quit accelerating, opened my eyes, and felt something indescribable—free fall.

For almost a minute, I was hurdling toward earth with no sensation other than floating. It was absolutely incredible. Then the parachute opened, and we maneuvered our way safely back to the landing strip. For the next hour or so, the three of us excitedly swapped stories of our jumps. What had felt like momentary death to me turned into one of the great exhilarations of my life.

Later it hit me. That's exactly what I had felt walking through the landmarks. The life I longed for had always been hidden underneath the death I feared. What was once an entrance into terror now held out the possibility for joy, and more joy.

And now it's up to you. The journey awaits you. But there is one final piece of advice I must give, and it may end up being the most helpful.

Jump.

AUTHOR INFORMATION

To get more information about Landmark Journey Ministries or to read Bill's blog, visit the website at landmarkjourneyministries.com

Bill is available as a speaker or retreat leader. To bring him to your event or organization, e-mail him at landmarkjourney@gmail.com

As a teacher, Bill enjoys feedback from others. You can join the discussion at facebook.com/LandmarkJourneyMinistries.

You can also follow Bill on Twitter @billdelvaux.